Leavenworth Papers   Number 18

Japan's Battle of Okinawa, April–June 1945

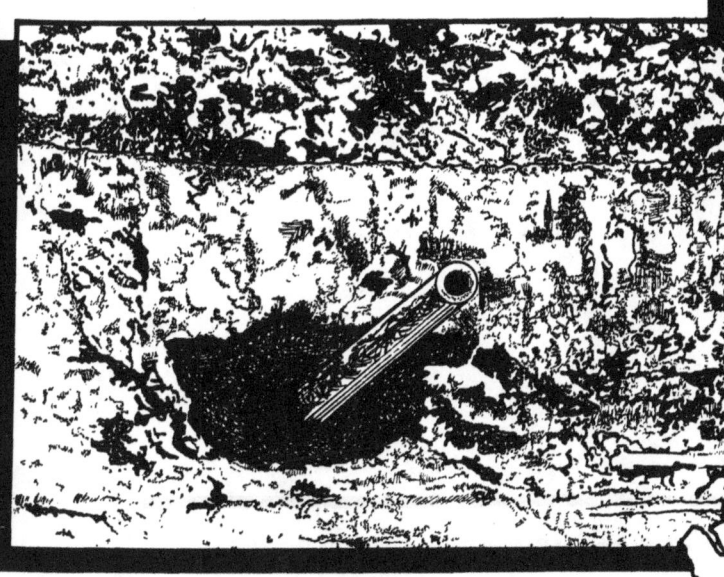

by Thomas M. Huber

Combat Studies Institute
U.S. Army Command and General Staff College
Fort Leavenworth, Kansas 66027-6900

Library of Congress Cataloging-in-Publication Data

Huber, Thomas M.
  Japan's battle of Okinawa, April to June 1945 / by Thomas M. Huber.
      p. cm.— (Leavenworth papers, ISSN 0195-3451 ; no. 18)
  Includes bibliographical references (p.   ).
  1. World War, 1939-1945—Campaigns—Japan—Okinawa Island.
I. Title. II. Series.
D767.99.045H83   1990   90-2223
940.54′25—dc20   CIP

For sale by the Superintendent of Documents, U.S. Government Printing Office, Washington, D.C. 20402

Contents

Illustrations v
Tables vii
Preface ix
Acknowledgments xi

Chapter

1. Anticipation of the Battle, March 1944 to March 1945 1
   Early Preparations: The Air Strategy 2
   IJA Main Units: Heavy and Light Divisions 14
   Other Units 16
   Reorganization 19
   The 32d Army's Leadership: Heroism Versus Realism 21
   The Locus of Authority in the 32d Army Staff 24
   Ground or Air 24

2. Defensive Engagement, April 1945 27
   The American Landings 27
   Planning the Japanese 12 April Offensive 31
   The American Advance 32
   The Japanese 12 April Offensive 32
   Night Problems 34
   Moving the Army North 35

3. Lethality in Motion: Tactics 41
   Cave Warfare 41
   The Command Cave 41
   Line and Artillery Caves 47
   Cave Warfare: Some Comparisons 63
   Okinawa Terrain 64
   Cave War Tactics 65
   Tanks Versus Caves 66
   Japanese Antitank Tactics 68
   American Anticave Tactics 71
   Japanese Artillery 74

4. Attack and Retreat, May 1945 81
   The 29 April Meeting 82
   Honorable Death Attack and Ritual Suicide 83
   Preparing the 4 May Offensive 84
   Results of the 4 May Offensive 86
   The 29 May Withdrawal 91

5. The Last Days, June 1945 105
   Japanese Casualties 118
   American Casualties 119
   Conclusion 120

Appendixes
   A 123
   B 125
Notes 131
Bibliography 141

Illustrations

Maps

1. The IJA 32d Army positions, August—November 1944 5
2. The IJA 32d Army positions, December 1944—Janaury 1945 8
3. The IJA 32d Army positions, January—March 1945 10
4. Movement of U.S. forces, 1—8 April 1945 28
5. Plan for the IJA's 12 April offensive 33
6. The IJA positions as of 25 April 1945 36
7. Plan for the IJA 4 May offensive 85
8. The IJA 4 May offensive 87
9. Preliminary withdrawal of the 62d Division, 25 May 1945 95
10. Withdrawal of the 24th Division, 29 May 1945 96
11. Withdrawal of the 44th Independent Mixed Brigade,
    31 May 1945 97
12. Final withdrawal of the 62d Division, 4 June 1945 98
13. The battle line on Oroku Peninsula, 4—13 June 1945 102
14. The IJA Kiyan line, 4 June 1945 106
15. Battle line on the Kiyan Peninsula, 10—19 June 1945 113

Figures

1. Organization of the IJA 24th Infantry Division, March 1945 15
2. Organization of the IJA 62d Infantry Division, March 1945 17
3. Organization of the 44th Independent Mixed Brigade
   and Kunigami Detachment 18
4. The Shuri command cave 42-43
5. Typical storage cave 48

v

6. Typical pillbox caves 50
7. An IJN 150-mm naval gun position 61
8. An IJA mortar position 62
9. Sleeve-type position 73

Tables

1. Average weekly battle casualties of American combat divisions on Okinawa for first two weeks of full engagement and for all subsequent weeks of full engagement 67

Preface

During the Pacific war, from 1937 to 1945, the Japanese military grew to an end strength of 7 million men. Over the course of the war, this represented some 28 million man-years of uniformed service to the Japanese Empire. Imperial service spanned every conceivable environment, from subarctic in Manchuria to steaming rain forest in New Guinea, and every conceivable adversary, from a Soviet armored corps at Nomonhan in 1939 to isolated nationalist guerrillas in the Philippine archipelago. Moreover, there is an abundant literature in Japanese on these experiences in the form of official histories, unit histories, memoirs, biographies, and studies by scholars and journalists. There is a rich harvest of military lessons that can be reaped from these extensive resources. Even so, this material has been left largely untouched by U.S. military theorists in the past because of the obstacle presented by the Japanese language.

Fortunately, for a time in the 1980s, Fort Leavenworth's Combat Studies Institute was able to foster research in these materials, of which this volume represents one product. I feel especially fortunate to have been associated with this effort.

THOMAS M. HUBER
Combat Studies Institute
U.S. Army Command and General Staff College

Acknowledgments

I wish to thank Dr. Roger Spiller, Dr. Edward Drea, Colonel Joseph Savittiere, and Dr. Gary Bjorge for their careful readings of early drafts of this manuscript and for the rich bounty of suggestions that they brought to it. I am grateful to Major Hara Tsuyoshi (JGSDF), currently of the Japanese National Institute for Defense Studies (JNIDS), for assisting me in my search for Okinawa veterans and Okinawa-related documents, to Captain Ito Koichi (IJA, Retired) for sharing with me some of his experiences on Okinawa, and to Professor Maehara Toru (JNIDS) for many useful insights into Imperial Japanese Army doctrine in World War II. I am indebted to Colonel Louis D. F. Frasché, Lieutenant Colonel John Hixson, and Lieutenant Colonel William Connor (all U.S. Army, Retired) for providing the congenial administrative environment in which this work was researched and written and to Colonel Richard Swain and Lieutenant Colonel Arthur Frame, who administratively expedited the editorial process. Finally, I greatly appreciate the efforts of Dr. Robert Berlin and Mrs. Marilyn Edwards, who energetically oversaw a myriad of production details, and of Mrs. Luella Welch, who retyped the manuscript in its later versions.

THOMAS M. HUBER
Combat Studies Institute
U.S. Army Command and General Staff College

Anticipation of the Battle, March 1944 to March 1945

The Battle of Okinawa, 1 April to 22 June 1945, is known to English-language readers through a variety of accounts, both official and commercial. Some of these works focus on operations, and some provide personal perspectives, so that most major features of the American experience on Okinawa are thoroughly known. However, another whole dimension of the Okinawa struggle is not as well known: Japan's Okinawa. To staff and line soldiers of the Imperial Japanese Army (IJA), the events of Okinawa appeared quite differently than they did to their American counterparts. For the Japanese, the operational problems were different, the solutions were different, and the perceived results from day to day were different. American combat experiences on Okinawa teach us something about the lethality of modern warfare; Japan's experiences on Okinawa may teach us still more.

The Japanese Empire's strategic need to hold Okinawa was absolute. After U.S. air strikes on Truk in February 1944, Imperial General Headquarters (IGHQ) assumed that the United States sooner or later would try to seize Okinawa as an advanced base for invading Japan itself and garrisoned the island with the newly organized 32d Army. As time went by, it became apparent that any U.S. assault on Okinawa would enjoy air superiority, artillery superiority, naval artillery cover, superior firepower on the line, and predominance in armor. Japan's 32d Army knew well in advance both where it would fight on Okinawa and that it would face overwhelming lethality.

Although the large Japanese garrison on Okinawa was as well supplied as it could be with men, provisions, and artillery, it was not well prepared at first with doctrine and training. Since Japan's Greater East Asian War began in 1937, its army had been conceived of and was a superior light infantry force. It relied on infiltration, maneuver, bold attack, and close combat to prevail over its lightly armed adversaries, the Chinese and European colonial garrisons. Beginning with Guadalcanal, however, Japan faced an adversary with more firepower than itself on limited island terrain. For an isolated Japanese island garrison subject to devastating offshore bombardment, maneuver and close combat skills were of little use. In fact, the IJA's received operational methods were completely inappropriate to the realities of most of the Pacific campaign, including Okinawa.

The latest trends in strategic doctrine being developed by IGHQ were also completely unsuitable as it turned out. IGHQ expected the defense of Okinawa to be achieved mainly by air power and envisioned Okinawa as a gigantic air base. In the eyes of IGHQ, 32d Army's mission was only to build the airstrips and then to provide service support for the air operations and security on the ground for the fields. In fact, however, severe shortages of planes and pilots made air defense of Okinawa unfeasible. The IJA's long-standing light infantry doctrine prescribed too little equipment for 32d Army at the same time that the new high-technology air strategy required far more state-of-the-art equipment than existed. The 32d Army was stranded between the two incompatible concepts.

How, then, did Japan's 32d Army cope with the problem of extreme lethality and its own doctrine's total inadequacy? The 32d Army Staff became locked in controversy over these problems, but in the end, ignoring their tradition and their superiors, they resolved to dig deep, contest the ground foot by foot, and use bold counterattack only selectively as an instrument of defense. Ultimately their methods resembled the fluid defense-in-depth tactics developed by German forces in World War I, though these methods would be used effectively here to oppose modern tanks and aircraft.

Early Preparations: The Air Strategy

The Okinawa campaign began for Americans on 1 April 1945, the day U.S. forces landed (L day). For the Japanese high command, however, the defense of Okinawa began over a year before. American air strikes against Truk in February 1944 made it clear to Japanese strategists that the Marianas line could fall, leaving the Ryukyu line as the main zone of defense. There then began a year of operational analysis, political maneuvering, reorganization, facilities development, and supply stockage that would determine as much as anything else the performance of Japanese forces on Okinawa. Japanese commentators sometimes leave the impression that these preparations were all important for the outcome and that the particular battle events were of minor consequence. Surviving staff officers were convinced that decisions made the year before L day critically affected what happened.

It was one of the peculiarities of the Okinawa campaign that the defenders knew long in advance the specific terrain where the battle was likely to be fought. Okinawa Island is only two to eighteen miles wide by sixty miles long—a small place for a violent clash of major powers, compared to, say, North Africa or the open Pacific. This battle area ensured that the fighting would be intense—densely packed forces supported by overwhelming firepower. These obvious facts conditioned the Japanese response.

In February 1944, just after the Truk air raids, IGHQ's "Outline of Preparations for the 'TEI-Go' Operation" provided for an increased defense presence in the area of the Ryukyu Islands and Taiwan. To this end IGHQ created the 32d Army headquarters late in March, to be located in Naha,

Okinawa. Its first commander, Lieutenant General Watanabe Masao, assumed his post on 1 April 1944, a year to the day before the Okinawa landings.[1]

The Ryukyus and Taiwan were to form a long zone of interprotective air bases under the TEI-Go and later plans. These bases were expected to defeat any American sea or air forces sent into the region. To avoid destruction from the air, each base was to consist of a cluster of airfields, such that if one were damaged others could be used immediately. Military and civilian crews were promptly set to work building the numerous fields. Thirteen base clusters had to be created, stretching in a line from Tachiarai in the northern Ryukyus to Pingting on Taiwan in the south.[2] IGHQ's extravagant scheme for the invulnerable air wall derived from its recent experiences on New Guinea. Japan's 4th Air Army there had no success destroying the Allied air base at Port Moresby because it consisted of six adjoining runways, protected by a dense radar and antiair net. IGHQ concluded that this same style of aviation fortress could effectively guard the Ryukyu line against naval approaches.[3]

The only remaining tasks for ground forces were the defense of these facilities and their support anchorages and the unenviable work of building the fields.[4] Much of the energy of 32d Army would be absorbed almost up to L day building these air facilities. This was the more difficult since 32d Army had only two bulldozers and one earth roller.[5] Japan had produced dozers in small numbers at its Komatsu plant since 1943, but few had reached the front. Since soldiers were thus obliged to use shovels, hoes, straw baskets, and horse-drawn wagons, construction was slow. Moreover, because of U.S. submarine raiders, it was impossible for the Japanese to deliver the large quantities of fuel, ammunition, and antiaircraft guns needed to operate the bases. Even more seriously, the planes themselves were not available.[6]

Tractor and rollers used by the Japanese on Okinawa

In May 1944, 32d Army had only enough forces to protect facilities on the island from small raids. The 32d Army Staff judged that American forces might assault Okinawa at any time in conjunction with a thrust into the Marianas or else might attack the Marianas first and not attack Okinawa until the spring of 1945. This meant that the 32d Army's Staff from the beginning lived with the apprehension of an immediate assault.[7]

IGHQ's TEI-Go plans were superseded in July 1944 by the SHO-Go plans in response to the loss of Saipan in that month. The several SHO-Go plans covered each area from northern Japan to the Philippines. The Philippines was covered by SHO-Go One and the Ryukyu area by SHO-Go Two. The plans called for 1,500 planes to swarm from China, Taiwan, and the Philippines in case U.S. forces entered the Ryukyu area.[8]

At the same time, noting the loss of Saipan, IGHQ began rushing major ground forces to Okinawa. The 15th Independent Mixed Regiment was sent immediately by air in July 1944. (The 15th would later be absorbed by the 44th Independent Mixed Brigade [IMB].) The other major units that were sent to Okinawa in July and August were the 24th Division, the 62d Division, the 9th Division, and the 44th IMB, all infantry. Infantry elements were also sent to Miyako, Ishigaki, Tokuno, Daito, and other neighboring islands.[9]

The premise at this time was that most U.S. forces would be destroyed on the water and that Japanese resources would be abundant. Therefore, 32d Army's strategy was to occupy all of Okinawa in force and to destroy the invasion party on whichever beach it appeared (see map 1). The 44th IMB was placed on Motobu Peninsula and Ie Island. The 24th Division was on the plain facing the Hagushi beaches. The 62d Division was on the narrow neck of land north of Urasoe-Mura, and the 9th Division held the landmass south of Urasoe-Mura. If the Americans landed at Itoman, the 24th and 62d Divisions were to move to the south. If they landed at Hagushi, the 9th and 62d Divisions were to move to the north.[10] The tendency of 32d Army Staff after the autumn of 1944, however, would be to increasingly compress these forces until almost all were deployed south of Uchitomari and to make their operational plans increasingly defensive.

The rapid buildup of ground forces from July to August 1944 occurred because IGHQ felt Okinawa might be a target immediately after Saipan. But with American landings on Palau and Leyte in September and October, IGHQ realized that the Philippines, not Okinawa, was the Americans' next objective. The fierce fighting on Leyte, under the rubric of SHO-Go One, affected 32d Army in several ways. Rigorous drilling of troops was begun, including divisional maneuvers to every conceivable American landing point. Night attacks on bridges were practiced. Staffs at all levels studied positions and strategy. At the end of October artillery units practiced bombarding beachheads with live shells, a demonstration that reassured the prefectural governor and civilian observers more than it did the 32d Army Staff. Even so, the rigorous training served to restore the troops' and officers' confidence, which had wavered in the face of the early news from Leyte.[11]

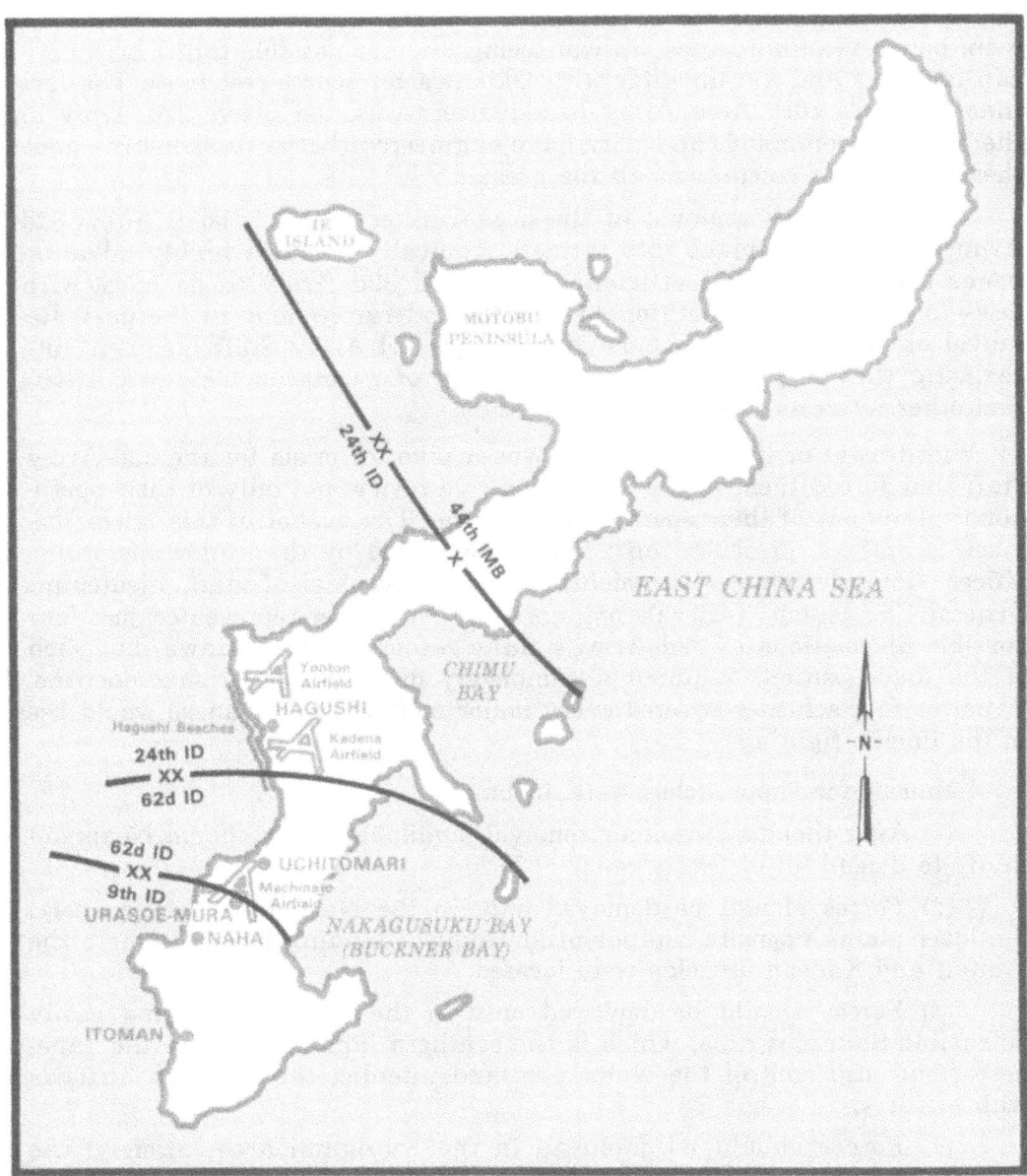

Map 1. The IJA 32d Army positions, August—November 1944

Unfortunately, it was at this time that IGHQ chose to withdraw the elite 9th Division from Okinawa to participate in the Leyte battle. On 13 November 1944, 32d Army Staff members received a telegram from IGHQ instructing them to designate their best division for redeployment to the Philippines, which staff members agreed was the 9th. The staff vigorously protested this removal of the 9th Division at the staff meeting in Taipei where it was discussed in early November, and continued to protest it right up to L day. Survivors protest it still. The 32d Army Staff's resentment over this was the greater since the 9th Division was actually sent to Taiwan, not to the Philippines, Taiwan being another possible target of American landings and a competitor with Okinawa for scarce resources. The fact that Taiwan's 10th Area Army headquarters was just above 32d Army in the chain of command, and may have engineered the move selfishly, made these feelings of resentment all the greater.[12]

The unexpected removal of the organization's best division threw 32d Army's operational plans into turmoil. Ironically it had a highly advantageous effect on combat efficiency. It forced 32d Army to do more with less—to economize—something IJA staffs had rarely done in the past. Removal of the 9th Division must have jolted 32d Army Staff members into realizing that they alone were the masters of events on Okinawa: IGHQ had other interests to pursue.

Withdrawal of the 9th Division was a pivot of crisis for the 32d Army Staff that forced them into a comprehensive review not only of their operational plans but of their operational doctrine. The upshot of this crisis was a set of options, presented on 23 November 1944 by the senior operations officer, Colonel Yahara Hiromichi, to 32d Army chief of staff, Lieutenant General Cho Isamu. Yahara's options of 23 November represented just four possible dispositions of 32d Army's finite resources on Okinawa, but each of the four positions required a completely different operational doctrine! Yahara's four schemes covered every major method the Japanese would use in the Pacific fighting.

Yahara's four approaches were, in brief:

(1) After the 9th Division's removal, available forces should be spread thinly to defend all of Okinawa.

(2) Forces should be deployed only in the Nakagami area, namely, the level plains opposite the potential Hagushi landing beaches where the Yontan and Kadena airfields were located.

(3) Forces should be deployed only in the mountainous and easily defensible Shimajiri area, which is the southern landmass where the Japanese could still control the Naha port and interdict the northern airfields with artillery.

(4) Forces should be deployed in the Kunigami area, namely, the mountainous areas in the far north that were easily defensible and did not invite attack because they had no strategic value.

In sum, 32d Army could attempt to defend all of Okinawa or only the center, only the south, or only the north.[13]

These four respective options corresponded, roughly speaking, to Japanese methods on (1) Guadalcanal, where contact with the main American force was piecemeal, (2) Saipan, where suicidal attack in the open brought early defeat, (3) Iwo Jima (still to take place), where there would be a dogged dug-in defense near airfields the Americans needed, and (4) Luzon (also still to come), where Japanese forces would withdraw to the northern mountains and survive to the end of the war intact but strategically passive.

Yontan airfield after rehabilitation by U.S. forces

Yahara's memorandum of 23 November 1944 rejected the first option, defense of all Okinawa, as no longer feasible for lack of forces, even though IGHQ favored it. He rejected the second option, defense of the open Hagushi plain, even though it might briefly protect the IGHQ's treasured airfields, because 32d Army would be immediately annihilated. He rejected the fourth option, cowering in the northern hills, even though it would keep the army unharmed, because in strategic terms, it would totally waste the resources over which the 32d Army Staff was the steward.[14]

Instead, Yahara endorsed the third option, concentrating all forces in the defensible but strategically critical south. Chief of Staff Cho agreed and passed the proposal to the 32d Army commander, Lieutenant General Ushijima Mitsuru, who without comment adopted it as 32d Army policy. Although this change in deployment seemed workaday, it actually entailed a massive and controversial change in 32d Army's operational doctrine. It meant abandoning the IJA's heretofore cherished policy of "decisive battle," namely, seeking out the enemy aggressively in close combat, in favor of a "war of attrition." It meant deliberately discarding the priority of antinaval air defense that for ten months had been, and still would be, the cornerstone of IGHQ's Pacific strategy. The 32d Army Staff's new commitment to attrition warfare in the south of the island was probably more important than any other event in making the IJA's performance on Okinawa, along with that on Iwo Jima, the most militarily effective of the Pacific war. The 32d Army Staff members were pleased with the new arrangement as a solid plan that would allow them to give a good account of themselves, and it was sent to the units on 26 November.[15]

The new plan contained five paragraphs. The 44th IMB was stationed on the Hagushi plain, the 62d Division was placed on the central isthmus, and the 24th Division was deployed on the southern end of the island (see

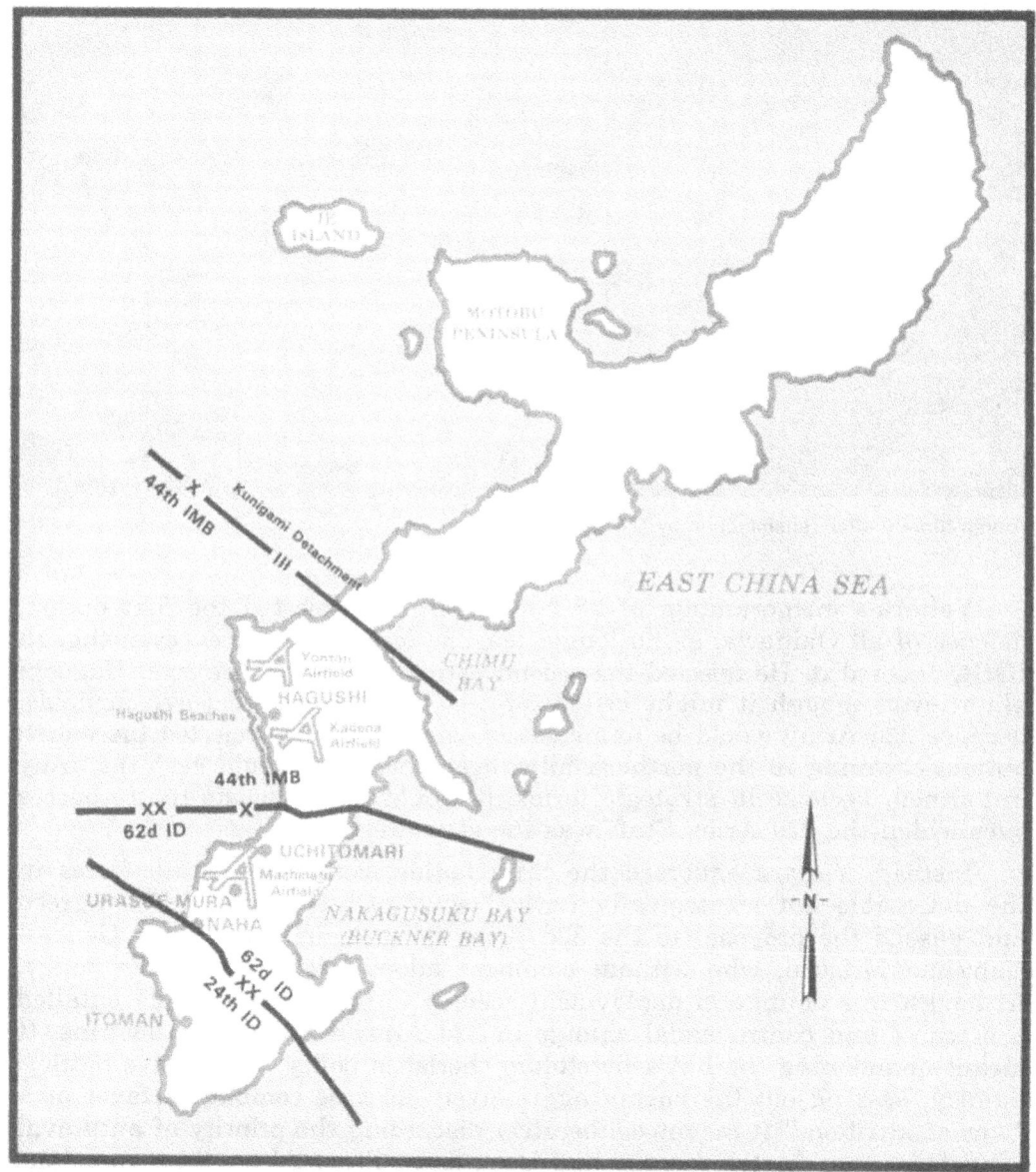

Map 2. The IJA 32d Army positions, December 1944—January 1945

map 2). The Kunigami Detachment was the only unit north of the Hagushi plain and on the Motobu Peninsula. The enemy "was to be contained by a strategic delaying action," not openly attacked for a "decisive battle." To placate IGHQ, the 44th IMB was placed in positions covering the Yontan and Kadena airfields. It was supposed to protect the fields as long as possible if the Americans landed at Hagushi and to counterattack them if the occasion offered. In reality, however, the 32d Army Staff intended for 44th IMB merely to harass the Americans and fall back southward toward the 62d Division's lines. The 32d Army Staff also expected 44th IMB to prevent early seizure of the airfields by American airborne troops.[16]

The 62d Division, on the central isthmus, was to repel possible American landings on the beaches near the Machinato airfield. It was also to prepare to fight on a line facing north if the Americans landed at Hagushi and to join the 24th Division if the Americans landed near Itoman. Similarly, the 24th Division was expected to help defend against landings north of Itoman and to join the 62d Division if there was fighting on the Machinato beaches or to the north.[17] In other words, the Americans were to be met with a solid front if they landed anywhere on the rugged isthmus or the southern landmass, but they were not to be engaged heavily if they landed on the open Hagushi plain. Moreover, in case of an attack at Itoman or Machinato, the Americans were to be fired on from the nearby mountains, then driven off the beaches in a "decisive battle." This was believed reasonably possible because the mountains extended near the shore, offering good defensive protection and also denying to the landing force the room it needed for staging.[18]

In December 1944 the commander of 10th Area Army on Taiwan, General Ando Rikichi, summoned 32d Army Chief of Staff Cho to Taipei to justify the new dispositions. Ando favored annihilating the Americans on the beaches as earlier doctrine required. He acquiesced in the new November dispositions, however, perhaps because he knew the 32d Army Staff was still resentful over the recent loss of the 9th Division, which was what had necessitated the November redeployment.[19]

The new force dispositions were carried out in December, and the new lines were inspected by Operations Officer Yahara in January. Yahara's prevalent impression, however, was that the defenses were too thin to hold against concentrated attack. IJA doctrine required no more than six miles of front per division. The 32d Army's two and one-half divisions were covering thirty-six miles of front, of which twenty-four miles had to be actively defended. Yahara concluded that the division fronts would have to be shortened, and that the way to do this was to draw 44th IMB from the Hagushi plain south to share some of the area covered by the 62d Division (see map 3). The new arrangement was endorsed by Cho and Ushijima and sent to the divisional units on 15 January 1945.[20]

The dispositions of 15 January would endure until the American landings on 1 April. They represented a culmination of the tendency of the 32d Army Staff, facing the prospect of American firepower, to shorten its lines

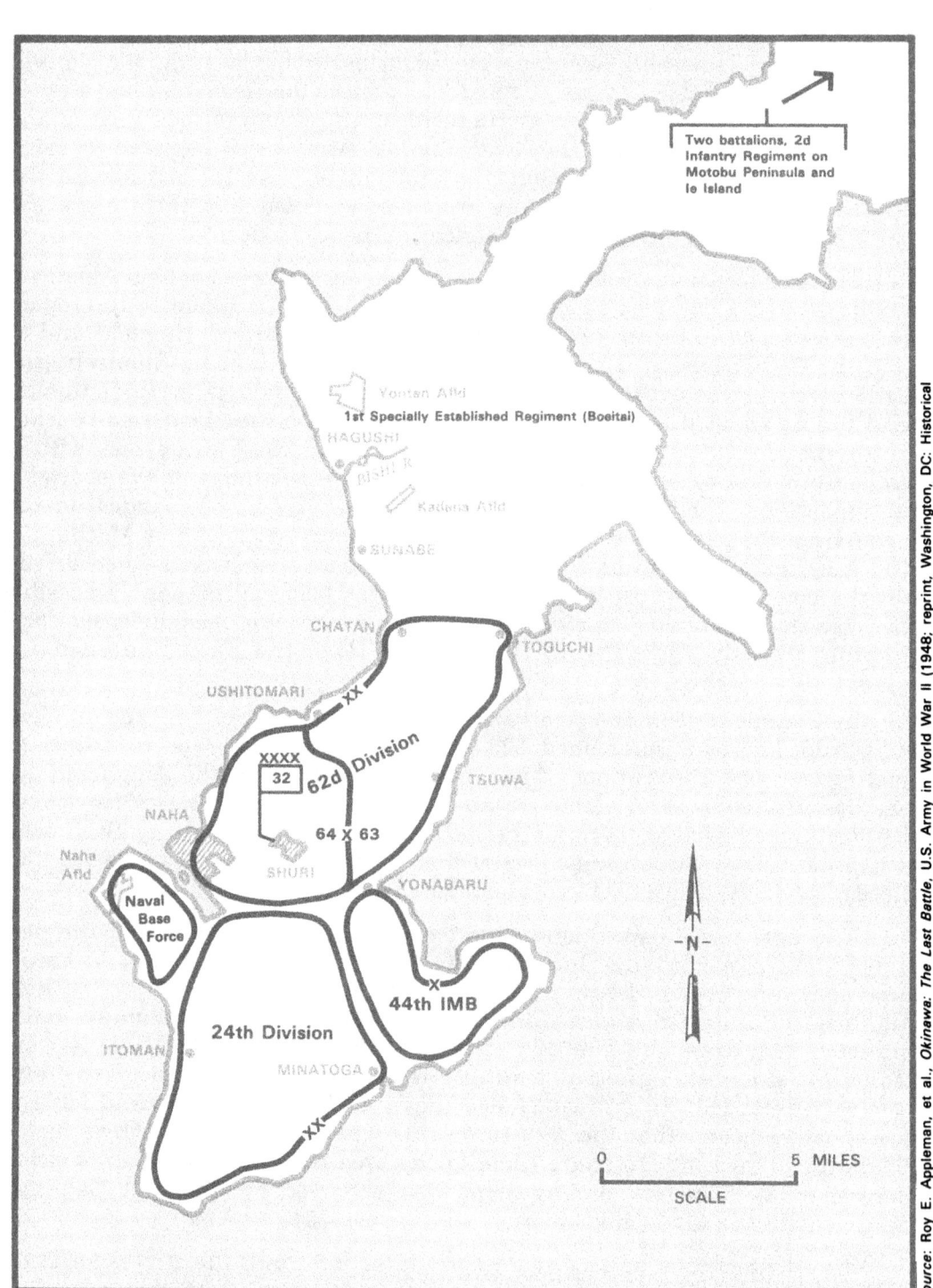

Map 3. The IJA 32d Army positions, January—March 1945

and give up its offensive plans. In the end 32d Army only defended the southernmost one-eighth of the island and abandoned the sought-after Yontan and Kadena airfields uncontested. In the eyes of IGHQ, Okinawa was part of a multitheater, technology-intensive strategy in which 32d Army's specialized role was to defend the Yontan and Kadena airfields. The 32d Army Staff members' perceptions were simpler: 32d Army was about to be attacked and needed defensible positions to survive. The staff members had no confidence that air forces could interdict the Americans and instead thought simply in terms of denying the Americans free use of Okinawa facilities as long as possible. Their larger strategic assumptions were well informed and in fact were more sound than the air power schemes of IGHQ. Even so, the staff's final operational plans amounted to nothing more nor less than denying the enemy the ground, foot by foot.

On 23 January 1944, 32d Army received a message from IGHQ saying that the 84th Division in Himeji would be sent to Okinawa to replace the 9th Division, which 32d Army had just lost, as indeed IGHQ had promised to do in November when the 9th Division was withdrawn. That same evening, however, the 32d Army Staff received a second message saying the dispatch of the 84th Division had been rescinded. Lieutenant General Miyazaki, head of the strategy branch of the IGHQ, claimed that he agonized over the decision but was ultimately reluctant to send forces from the home islands when Japan itself might soon be under attack. Reasonable as this was, the decision did nothing for the morale of the forces on Okinawa and merely confirmed their conviction that IGHQ was not going to send them the resources they needed.[21]

Staff officers on Okinawa felt that their headquarters had abandoned them and that, eventually, they would be overwhelmed and destroyed by the Americans. They expected the Americans to land six to ten divisions against the Japanese garrison of two and a half divisions. The staff calculated that superior quality and numbers of weapons gave each U.S. division five or six times the firepower of a Japanese division. This meant that U.S. firepower on the ground would be twelve times Japanese firepower or more. To this would be added the Americans' abundant naval and air firepower. Understandably, January 1945 was a time of dark thoughts and sullen inaction for the 32d Army Staff.[22]

To alleviate this mood, Operations Officer Yahara prepared a pamphlet titled "The Road to Certain Victory" in which he argued that, through the use of fortifications, 32d Army could defeat the Americans' superior numbers and technology. Building and using tunnels, what he called "sleeping tactics," was the method he recommended as suitable and capable of success. Chief of Staff Cho deleted the few lines that were pessimistic and then had the pamphlet printed and distributed. The pamphlet's purpose was to get the troops and officers stirred up enough to work on their fortifications, which they now did in an environment of renewed optimism.[23]

Work on the caves now began with great vigor. "Confidence in victory will be born from strong fortifications" was the soldiers' slogan. The caves meant personal shelter from the fierce bombardments that were sure to come, and they also offered a shimmering hope of victory. The combination was irresistible, and units began to work passionately on their own caves. Moreover, after frequent relocation, the units were finally in the positions where they would remain until the Americans landed. The 62d Division and the 24th Division would be in their final positions 100 days and the 44th IMB 50 days before L day.[24]

Enthusiasm was essential because of the great toil it took to create the caves. Just as 32d Army had only two bulldozers to make airfields, it had no mechanized tunneling equipment at all. Chief of Staff Cho repeatedly requested such equipment, so often, in fact, that "Cho's rock-cutters" became famous in the corridors of IGHQ. Still, none were sent. In lieu of cutting machines, the soldiers used trenching tools and shovels.[25]

Besides lacking cutting equipment, 32d Army lacked construction materials. It had no cement, no ironware, and no dynamite. The units had to rely entirely on wooden beams that they obtained themselves to shore up their shafts. This was not necessarily easy because there were no forests in the south of the island where the troops were now stationed. Pine forests were abundant in the mountainous north, however, so each unit was assigned its own lumbering district in the north. Several hundred men from each division were detailed as its lumbering squad. The problem remained, however, of how to move the several million logs that were needed over the forty or so miles from the forests to the forts. There was no railroad, and although 32d Army had trucks, the 10 October air raids on Naha had destroyed most of the gasoline. The trucks, therefore, could not be used for the vast work of moving the logs. The solution was for each unit to cut its own logs, then transport them in small native boats called *sabenis*. The divisions acquired seventy of these, which then plied the waters steadily from north to south. In January 1945, however, the Leyte-based B-24s that began flying over daily for reconnaissance also began strafing the boats. So the waterborne delivery of logs had to be switched from day to night, greatly lowering efficiency.[26]

Other problems cave builders found had to do with the quality of the soil. Local geological conditions made it possible for the finished tunnel positions to be highly resistant to fire, although these same conditions made building the tunnels difficult. The whole island south of Futema consisted of coral stone that was thirty to sixty feet thick and as hard as concrete. (This was not the case in the north, which was one of the reasons Yahara had seen fit to abandon the north in November.) Digging through the coral took tremendous toil, and soldiers wore their picks and trenching tools to stumps. Once through the coral crust, however, the earth was a soft red clay, relatively easy to penetrate. Besides that, there were natural caves in each area of the south that soldiers could take over and expand. Some of the natural caves could accommodate 1,000 men each. Soldiers felt the thick coral crust was as good as a ferroconcrete lid for their caves, and indeed the caves would protect their inhabitants completely from bomb and shell.[27]

The 32d Army intended to, and did, move its entire force underground. The caves were made large enough to hold all personnel, weapons, ammunition, provisions, and "all other material." Prior to November 1944 each unit had been expected to fashion its caves for three times its own numbers so that troops from other areas could be concentrated in any area and remain underground. This more ambitious goal had to be abandoned in November 1944, however, when the major troop shifts reduced the number of working days in each unit's new sector. Still, 32d Army built sixty miles of the underground fortifications.[28]

The 32d Army devised elaborate antitank construction plans. A system of antitank trenches was to be built. In addition there were to be foxholes on likely tank routes, antitank minefields, and the blockade and destruction of major tank routes. The projected antitank trench system was especially ambitious. Almost no progress was made building it, however, because 32d Army was obliged to devote its leftover construction energies to IGHQ's airfields.[29]

The 32d Army strove to strengthen personnel structure as well as its physical fortifications. It evacuated a portion of Okinawa's population of 435,000 to the main Japanese islands, partly for their safety and partly to prevent their consuming precious foodstuffs once communications with the outside were cut off. Eighty thousand Okinawans were moved to Kyushu on munitions vessels that were otherwise returning to Japan empty. Because transportation was scarce and the inhabitants reluctant, however, the army also began moving Okinawans from the populous southern half of the island, which was going to be contested, to the safer north. Thirty thousand old people and children were moved to the north by mid-March 1945, and 30,000 more when U.S. landings became imminent.[30]

The 32d Army Staff also wished to use as much of the indigenous population as it could in direct support of the war effort, so on 1 January 1945 it ordered total mobilization. All Okinawan males aged 18 to 45 were obliged to enter the Japanese service. Thirty-nine thousand were drafted, of whom 15,000 were used as nonuniformed laborers and 24,000 as rear-echelon troops called the Home Guard (*Boeitai*). Many of the *Boeitai* replaced sea based battalions and rear-area supply units that had been reorganized and equipped for frontline duty.[31]

In addition to these, 1,500 of the senior boys of the middle schools on Okinawa were organized into Iron and Blood Volunteer Units and assigned to frontline duty. Some of these students had been tried out in the signal service in the autumn of 1944 with good results, so the program was expanded. Since the fall of 1944, 600 senior students of the girls' middle schools also had been given training in the medical service.[32]

Okinawa's economy produced sweet potatoes to feed the cows and pigs, and imported rice from Taiwan to feed the human population. The 32d Army resolved that the livestock would be slaughtered for food and that the populace and army would subsist on the sweet potatoes, thus making the island self-sufficient in food. (Replacing rice with sweet potatoes, the poor man's food, was distasteful to soldier and civilian alike for cultural reasons.) The 32d Army went further and produced alcohol from the sweet potatoes for use as auto and truck fuel, at the rate of 300 drums a month.[33]

IJA Main Units: Heavy and Light Divisions

The principal army units on hand as of March 1945 were 32d Army headquarters, 24th Infantry Division, 62d Infantry Division, and 44th Independent Mixed Brigade, plus 5th Artillery Command and 27th Tank Regiment. In addition to these were some sixty antiair, machine-gun, and engineering units ranging from battalion to company size. The largest of these was the so-called 11th Shipping Group, whose 19 units boasted some 9,000 men, most of them in Sea Raiding Base Battalions, meaning that their job was to send one-man motorboats filled with explosives against the invasion fleet.[34]

The 32d Army headquarters was itself a formidable force with 7,075 men. Of these, 1,070 were in the headquarters itself, to which were attached 1,912 in a signal regiment, 204 in an army hospital, 1,167 in a field freight depot, and so on. The 32d Army was formed by IGHQ on 22 March 1944 as the main command unit for Okinawa. From 11 August 1944, it was commanded by Lieutenant General Ushijima Mitsuru and based in Naha.[35]

The first of the main combat units to reach Okinawa was the 24th Division, a heavy division. It was organized in December 1939, assigned to 32d Army on 18 July 1944, and disembarked on Okinawa from Manchuria on 5 August 1944. Its commander was Lieutenant General Amamiya Tatsumi. The 24th, a triangular division with three regiments, three battalions per regiment, and three companies per battalion, was organized and equipped for strategic warfare against mechanized and well-armed Russian forces of the sort the IJA clashed with at Nomonhan in 1939. It had abundant combat support units, with artillery, engineer, transport, and reconnaissance elements organic at regimental level. Each regiment, battalion, and company had its own artillery unit, and each battalion also boasted an antitank gun company. The transport regiment included three motor transport companies. In a word, the 24th, with its firepower, mobility, specialization, and consistent triangular structure was fashioned for large-scale operations with another modern army (see figure 1).[36]

Very different from the 24th was the 62d Division, a light division. The 62d was formed in June 1943 in Shansi, China; was assigned to 32d Army on 24 July 1944; was concentrated at Shanghai from North China on 13 August 1944; left Shanghai on 16 August; and disembarked at Naha on 19 August. Commanded by Lieutenant General Fujioka Takeo, the 62d was a pentagonal division with a proliferation of small autonomous rifle units and little else. It had two brigades, with five battalions per brigade and five rifle companies per battalion. Although it had engineer, medical, and signal units at division level, it had no organic artillery above company level, little firepower, and little mechanized transport. The 62d Division was

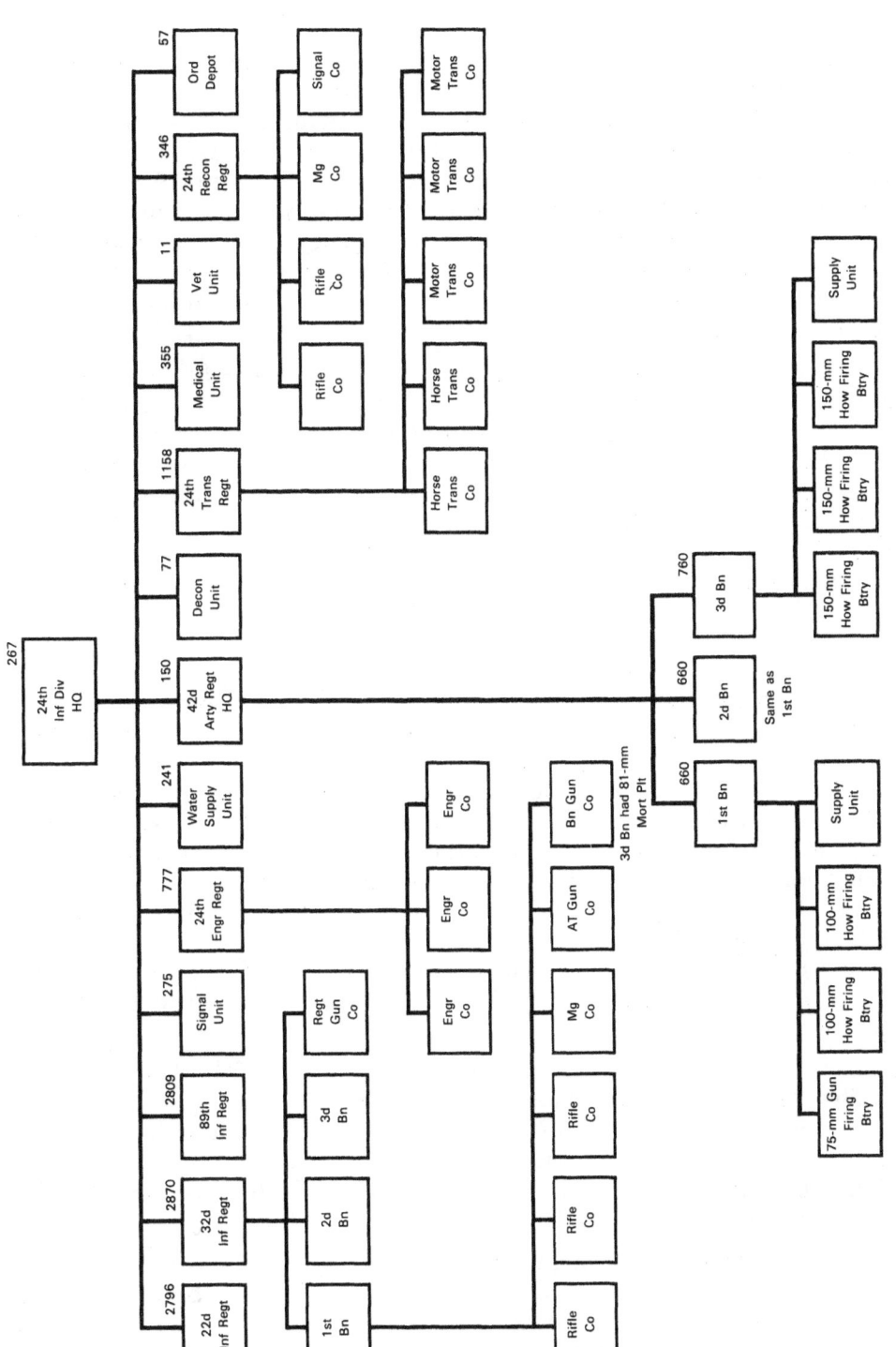

Source: Charles S. Nichols and Henry I. Shaw, *Okinawa: Victory in the Pacific* (Washington, DC: Historical Branch, G-3 Division, U.S. Marine Corps, 1955), 57.

Figure 1. Organization of the IJA 24th Infantry Division, March 1945

really just ten clusters of rifle companies, a very light division (see figure 2).[37]

The 62d Division was so different in concept from the highly structured, heavily equipped 24th Division that it might have belonged to an entirely different army. In fact, it did belong to a different army. The 24th Division had been organized by the Kwantung Army to face Soviet armor on the Manchurian plain shortly after the Nomonhan incident in 1939. The 62d Division, on the other hand, had been organized by the Central China Expeditionary Army for use as a counterinsurgency force and antilight infantry force. It was the only major unit to have seen action before Okinawa, and during most of its service, its two brigades had been autonomous and not part of a division at all.

In reality, 24th Division was organized to face state-of-the-art Russian armored columns in Manchuria, but 62d Division was organized to fight furtive rural guerrillas in China. These two military tasks were so different that the Japanese army headquarters responsible had evolved completely different organizational structures for their constituent divisions. In the event, of course, the lethal Okinawa battleground would present challenges that resembled neither the mechanized war of the north nor the guerrilla war of the south.[38]

Other Units

The third major combat unit that would fight on Okinawa was the 44th Independent Mixed Brigade, commanded by Major General Suzuki Shigeki. The 44th IMB was organized on Kyushu, but its headquarters, 2d Infantry Regiment, brigade artillery, and engineering units were sunk by a U.S. submarine while en route to Okinawa on 29 June 1944. These elements were thus reconstituted between July and September and dispatched again, this time more successfully. The 15th Independent Mixed Regiment was formed on Okinawa on 6–12 July 1944 by airlift from Japan. It was assigned to the 44th IMB on 22 September 1944. Both the 2d Infantry Regiment and the 15th Independent Mixed Regiment portions of the 44th IMB were triangular in organization, with artillery units attached at every level from company up (see figure 3).[39]

Artillery on Okinawa was concentrated under the 5th Artillery Command. The 5th Artillery was about brigade sized, with 5,300 men. It included, besides its headquarters, four artillery regiments and three mortar battalions. The artillery regiments used 150-mm howitzers and 150-mm cannons. The 1st Independent Artillery Mortar Regiment had twenty-four 320-mm spigot mortars.[40]

The lavish artillery arrangements were due to the efforts of Operations Officer Yahara, who had asked IGHQ for the guns and for the 5th Artillery Command to control them. Yahara intended to conceal all the artillery in the center of the southern defense positions so that all of 32d Army's firepower could be concentrated at once on any part of the front that might be engaged. Though 32d Army had far less artillery than the Americans, it

17

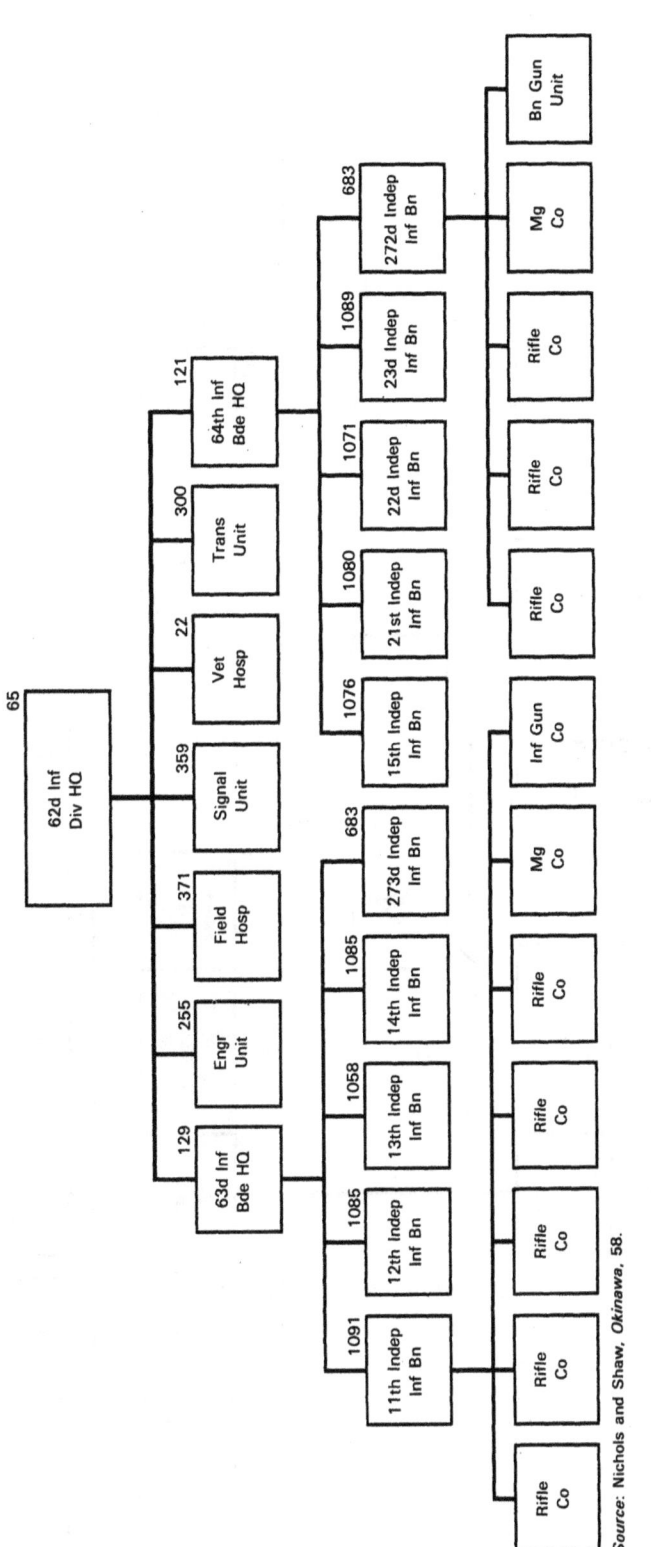

Source: Nichols and Shaw, *Okinawa*, 58.

Figure 2. Organization of the IJA 62d Infantry Division, March 1945

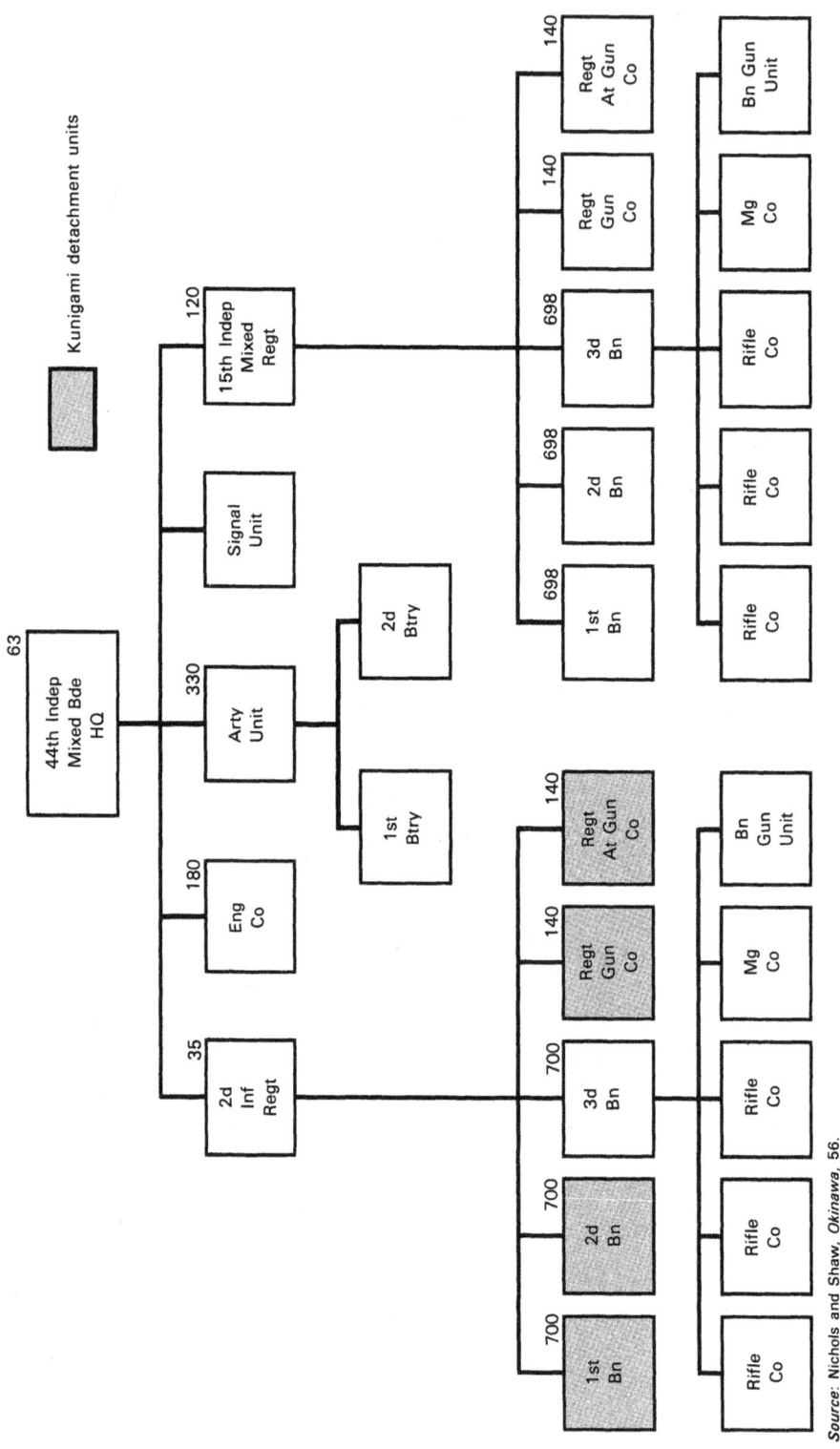

Figure 3. Organization of the 44th Independent Mixed Brigade and Kunigami Detachment

could in this way get the maximum effect from what it did have. To direct this ambitious project Yahara requested and got the noted artillerist Lieutenant General Wada Kojo.[41]

The 5th Artillery Command's headquarters (almost 150 officers and troops) was assigned to Okinawa on 22 August 1944 and arrived there on 22 October. The subordinate regiments, some of which came from Japan and some from Manchuria, arrived at various times between July and December.[42] The only armored unit that the 32d Army had was the 27th Tank Regiment of 750 men. The regiment, consisting of a medium tank company with fourteen tanks, a light tank company with thirteen tanks, a tractor-drawn artillery battery, an infantry company, a maintenance company, and an engineering platoon, arrived in Okinawa from Manchuria on 12 July 1944.[43]

Besides the main line units, there were several independent specialized commands that answered directly to the 32d Army headquarters, including the 21st Antiaircraft Artillery Command with its seven antiaircraft battalions, the 11th Shipping Group with several shipping engineer regiments and sea-raiding battalions, the 19th Air Sector Command that supervised assorted aviation service units, and the 49th Line of Communications Command with several independent motor transport companies. Besides these units, there were four independent machine-gun battalions, four independent antitank battalions, and an independent engineer battalion that were parceled out as needed to the main line units.[44]

The Imperial Japanese Navy (IJN) had almost 9,000 men at the Oroku Naval Air Base adjacent to Naha. Of these, 3,400 were in the Okinawa Naval Base Force and others in various maintenance or construction units. Among the naval units, only the 150 troops in the 81-mm mortar battery had been trained for ground combat prior to arriving in Okinawa. The naval forces, under Rear Admiral Ota Minoru, were to be under army jurisdiction once the Americans landed.[45]

Reorganization

The total strength of the Japanese forces on Okinawa was about 100,000; 67,000 of these were in the IJA, 9,000 were in the IJN, and 24,000 were impressed Okinawans used mostly in service support roles. The strengths of the IJA main units were 32d Army headquarters, 1,070; 32d Army direct service units, 6,005; 24th Division, 14,360; 62d Division, 11,623; and 44th IMB, 4,485. These units accounted for only 38,000 of the IJA's 67,000-man complement, however. The remaining 29,000 men were in the specialized antiaircraft, sea-raiding, and airfield battalions.[46]

It occurred to the 32d Army Staff, however, that these richly manned service units should be reorganized for ground combat, given the anticipated nature of the coming struggle. Between 13 and 20 February 1945, the 1st, 2d, 3d, 26th, 27th, 28th, and 29th Sea-Raiding Base Battalions were restructured and became the 1st, 2d, 3d, 26th, 27th, 28th, and 29th Independent Battalions. By February, these seven battalions' motorboat bases had already been built, and the base forces of 900 men each had little to do. Therefore, only motorboat pilot and maintenance companies were left at the bases, and the remaining 600 men per battalion were withdrawn for use as light infantry battalions. Each independent battalion had three companies of 150 to 180 men each, and their men were already trained and furnished with rifles and grenades. To this was added only four light machine guns and two heavy grenade launchers apiece. The seven independent battalions, with about 4,500 troops altogether, were then distributed to the 24th and 62d Divisions and to the 44th IMB.[47]

On 21 March, 32d Army Staff issued an order that reorganized almost all service support units for ground combat and placed them under the command of the 62d and 24th Divisions. The 19th Air Sector Command, for example, became the 1st Specially Established Regiment and was assigned to defend, under 62d Division, the same Yontan and Kadena airfields it had recently built and maintained.[48]

The 1st Specially Established Brigade was created from elements of the 49th Line of Communications Command and placed under that unit's headquarters commander. It consisted of the 2d, 3d, and 4th Specially Established Regiments and was made up of line of communications, field ord-

Special attack (*kamikaze*) motorboats prepared by the Japanese for use on Okinawa

nance depot, and field freight depot units respectively. It was stationed in the Naha-Yonabaru area under the command of the 62d Division.[49]

The 2d Specially Established Brigade was created under the 11th Shipping Group commander. Its 5th and 6th Specially Established Regiments were drawn from leftover sea raiders and Home Guards (native Okinawans drafted and put in military units) and elements of the 11th Shipping Group respectively. The 2d Specially Established Brigade was stationed on the southwestern end of Okinawa under the command of the 24th Division.[50]

This reorganization of 21 March added 14,000 men to ground combat strength, leaving only 10,500 of the 67,000 IJA force in specialized service roles. Even among these 10,500, the 3,000 men of the seven antiaircraft battalions were assigned antitank and other direct-fire artillery roles on the infantry line once hostilities began. This entailed line use of seventy 7.5-mm antiaircraft guns and 100 antiaircraft automatic cannons.[51]

The 9,000 IJN troops on Oroku were also reorganized for ground combat at the end of March. This force was oriented almost entirely to naval and naval air activities. The 13-mm and 25-mm antiaircraft batteries in the Okinawa Naval Base Force were able to convert their guns easily for ground service as direct-fire weapons. But this and other naval units suffered from a lack of appropriate infantry equipment, especially individual weapons, as well as from a complete lack of training for ground fighting. Even so, the Oroku force was all reorganized into battalions headed by naval lieutenants and companies headed by lieutenants junior grade.[52]

In short, as the battle approached in February and March of 1945, 4,500 men from sea-raiding units, 14,000 men from various shipping and communications units, and 3,000 men from antiaircraft units, a total of 21,500 men of the 29,000 not already in major line units, were reorganized for potential service on the infantry line. To this total, 9,000 naval troops were also added. Almost all these units were light infantry, however, armed only with rifles and the few machine guns and mortars 32d Army had to distribute. These units were not trained for infantry combat, and many of their troops remained in rear-area auxiliary roles until late in the battle when the original line units were badly depleted.

The 32d Army's Leadership: Heroism Versus Realism

The individual personalities on an army staff, despite their influence on the outcome of battle, are often forgotten. This was not the case in the IJA 32d Army, however. In the 32d Army Staff, two very different tendencies were present, each represented by a highly placed staff member. The entire strategy of the Okinawa battle on the Japanese side was worked out by the interaction of these two officers' factions and their conflicting policies. Who were the leading lights of the 32d Army Staff, and what strategic principles did they represent?

The 32d Army commander was Lieutenant General Ushijima Mitsuru, who was appointed on 8 August 1944 and arrived at his post two days later.[53] By a routine command rotation, he replaced Lieutenant General

Lieutenant General
Ushijima Mitsuru,
commander, 32d Army

Watanabe Masao, who had been commander since 32d Army's inception on 22 March 1944. Ushijima graduated from the Japanese Military Academy (JMA) at Zama in 1908, was a former vice minister in the Ministry of the Army, and had been an infantry commander in Burma early in the war. In 1944 he was serving as commandant of the Japanese Military Academy. He was a quiet commander who ordinarily approved whatever policy his staff presented to him. His chosen role was to provide moral support to subordinates and if need be to help them reach agreement and resolve differences. In sum he was a transcendent leader in the mainstream of the Japanese tradition. He would not become embroiled in the disputes that divided the 32d Army Staff but would at times help to mend them.[54]

The man with overall responsibility for 32d Army's day-to-day operations was its chief of staff, Lieutenant General Cho Isamu (JMA, 1916). Cho had had an extraordinary career. As a captain in 1930, he had belonged to the right-wing extremist Cherry Society. He was involved in several attempted military coups d'etat, including one in October 1931 in which he agreed to become chief of the Tokyo police if the coup succeeded. For his involvement in this episode, he was sent to Manchuria, and later in 1938, he took part in the clash with Soviet forces at Lake Khasan, near the northeast Korean border, and did some of the negotiating with the

IJA 32d Army Staff in early February 1945. In the front row are (1) Lieutenant General Ushijima Mitsuru, (2) Lieutenant General Cho Isamu, and (3) Colonel Yahara Hiromichi

Russians. He won fame throughout the IJA by dozing on a hillside with great snores in plain view of the Soviet enemy.

In early 1944 Cho was brought from the general headquarters of the Kwantung Army to Tokyo to participate in the projected recapture of Saipan. When IGHQ abandoned that idea on 27 June, it sent him to Okinawa on 1 July to analyze the strategic situation. On 5 July he wired IGHQ that Okinawa needed three divisions to protect it, plus 30,000 bags of cement for building extensive cave fortifications. These requests may or may not have been prompted by the staff already on Okinawa, but they did conform closely to the main outlines of actual defense arrangements later. In any case Cho was appointed chief of staff of the 32d Army on 8 July 1944.[55]

Cho drank generously and when intoxicated would perform a dance with his samurai sword. He liked having fine cuisine and good scotch in his headquarters. He was enthusiastic and communicated that enthusiasm to those around him. He harbored strong resentments against those who crossed him, but only briefly. In short he was a man of strong feeling and aggressive personality who believed infinitely in his cause and in the capabilities of the IJA. He also tended to base strategic judgments on his enthusiasms rather than on a cool appreciation of reality.[56]

Cho's chief subordinate was the senior operations officer, Colonel Yahara Hiromichi (JMA, 1923). Yahara had been with the 32d Army since its inception on 22 March 1944 and prior to that had attended the Japanese War College; served ten months at Fort Moultrie in the United States; served as a staff officer in China, Malaya, and Burma; and taught at the JMA. By personality and inclination he was the opposite of Cho. He was seen by colleagues as introspective and aloof but good at his business, which was crafting operations. For him war was a science whose practice demanded cool rationality. When Cho was made Yahara's superior on 8 July, there was some soul-searching among the IGHQ staff as to whether that was a good idea, but the staff at last decided it was.[57]

In the event, Yahara and Cho would often have different views on what operations should be carried out, with the rest of the 32d Army Staff supporting one man or the other. The two men had very different assumptions about the nature of ground combat and what factors were most important in determining its outcome. Observing the drama between Cho and Yahara and throwing the consensual weight of the headquarters one way or the other was the rest of 32d Army Staff: six lieutenant colonels and majors on the central staff of 32d Army who were privy to the main operational decisions, as well as four colonels and a major who headed weapons, administration, medical, and legal branches of the 32d Army headquarters (see appendix A).[58]

The Locus of Authority in the 32d Army Staff

IJA staffs did not reach decisions in the same manner as U.S. Army staffs. In the U.S. Army, a unit commander would hear the evidence from his staff, then decide on a course of action. In the IJA, however, unit commanders had only a symbolic function. The commander was expected only to carry the burden of spiritual responsibility on his shoulders, manage contacts between his unit and superiors, and offer moral support to his subordinates. Practical responsibility for the unit as a whole lay in the hands of its chief of staff. Tasks relating to operations were delegated to the senior staff officer, whose position was similar to a U.S. G3 but who had far more influence than his U.S. counterpart because of the commander's passivity. When trying to arrive at an operational decision, the rest of the staff was expected to provide information and insights and to discuss the issue at hand in the context of a staff meeting. The chief of staff would articulate the policy chosen, and then the whole staff was supposed to agree by consensus that the course chosen was right. The senior staff officer would then draw up the plans and oversee their implementation.

Compared to American practice, this system gave more power to the staff, especially the junior members, and meant that staff discussions tended to shape more directly the content of command decisions. The commander himself was aware of the issues and was present at staff meetings to bless the results, but ordinarily he did not intervene as long as the decision-making process was working. These unique IJA staff practices sprang in part from the German example, which had been influential in the IJA's formative decades, and in part from indigenous traditions of consensus decision making. In the Okinawa campaign, these practices governed the staff-meeting environment in which crucial decisions were reached in a struggle of words between Cho and Yahara.

Ground or Air

In March 1945, 32d Army requested that IGHQ allow the destruction of the Yontan and Kadena airfields on the grounds that the airfields were impossible to defend. A brigade could delay their seizure for no more than several days and then only at the cost of thousands of lives. Therefore, 32d Army argued, it was better to destroy the airfields, which would deny their use to the enemy for ten days at no cost of life. IGHQ approved the request, so destruction began on 10 March 1945 "using the air units in the area" and was largely completed by the end of the month.[59]

Destroying the airfields marked a dramatic turnaround of IGHQ's earlier policy. Prior to this time IGHQ had expected the defense of Okinawa to be accomplished mainly by air power and had envisioned Okinawa as a giant air base complex. In this, IGHQ had been at odds with the 32d Army Staff from the beginning. The 32d Army, expecting imminent American landings, saw Okinawa in terms of a land-based defense. It had no confidence that Japanese air power would have the desired effect of limiting the American approach.

IGHQ, on the other hand, under its TEI-Go plan of April to July 1944 saw Okinawa only as an air base to help defend the Marianas line. Under the SHO-Go plan of July to November 1944, which recognized the need for ground defense of Okinawa, it was still assumed that many of the invading Americans would be stopped in the water by 1,500 suicide planes gathered for that purpose in China, Taiwan, and the Philippines. Even the TEI-Go plans of November 1944 to April 1945 still laid heavy emphasis on the use of suicide air attacks against the U.S. fleet, albeit launched from Kyushu and Taiwan, not Okinawa. The 32d Army's Yahara felt this air-oriented policy, which built airfields without protecting them, was tantamount to building airfields for the enemy.[60]

In July and August 1944 Cho and Yahara, from their vantage point on Okinawa, were doubtful of the efficacy of Japanese air power and directed all the energies of their then just-arriving main units to building fortifications. The building of airfields, IGHQ's priority, was left to Okinawan laborers. During August 1944, IGHQ sent several emissaries of lieutenant general rank to Okinawa to inspect the airfields' progress. When the pace was discovered to be slow, they severely castigated Cho and threatened to dissolve the whole 32d Army Staff. Faced with this eventuality, Cho finally did devote enough resources to building the airfields so that they were mostly completed by the end of September 1944.[61]

When the 44th IMB withdrew from the Hagushi plain in February 1945—leaving Yontan and Kadena airfields unprotected—the 6th Air Army, the element of 10th Area Army on Taiwan responsible for Okinawa's air defense, complained bitterly. The 32d Army asked for more troops if it had to defend the airfields, but was denied. A compromise was worked out with IGHQ whereby 32d Army was permitted to interdict American use of the airfields by long-range artillery fire.[62] On the other hand, the 32d Army wished to have a number of suicide attack planes based on Okinawa to strike the U.S. fleet suddenly when it came within sixty miles. IGHQ promised 32d Army 300 planes for this, but the delivery schedule fell behind and few planes were actually available when the landing day came.[63]

Throughout the long period of waiting, March 1944 to March 1945, IGHQ relied on an air strategy that assumed abundant supplies and equipment would be available. But the strategy became increasingly implausible as time went by, especially to the 32d Army Staff members, who knew what had happened on Saipan and on Iwo Jima and who knew the outcomes of the air battles of the Philippine Sea and of Taiwan. For IGHQ to reverse its policy at the eleventh hour, early March 1945, meant that in the end even IGHQ recognized that an air defense strategy was hopeless and that Okinawa would have to be held by fighting on the ground. Reliance on high-technology air power to avoid a decisive encounter on the ground proved a fantasy, a fantasy appreciated first by ground officers in the area about to be overrun.

Defensive Engagement, April 1945

By the end of March, 32d Army was fairly well prepared to resist invasion, although a last-minute personnel shuffle interfered with unit cohesion. The U.S. preparatory bombardment soon began. On 23 March 1945, American carrier planes bombed Okinawa, and on 24 March, a preparatory naval bombardment rained down 13,000 6- and 16-inch shells. These fires had no specific targets, however, and amounted to little more than area fire. The 32d Army's concealment had been so effective that, despite daily aerial reconnaissance, the American gunners did not know where on the island it was.[1]

On 26 March, American forces secured the Kerama Islands, sixty miles west of Naha, and placed eight 105-mm guns there. The Japanese went to "War Preparations A"—namely, full readiness. The few available *kamikaze* aircraft on Okinawa sortied from Kadena airfield on 27, 28, and 29 March and damaged some American ships.[2] To raise morale, Lieutenant General Cho put up a sign next to the 32d Army command cave that read "Heaven's Grotto Battle Headquarters," a lighthearted reference to the national foundation myth. What really raised morale, however, was that the arduously constructed cave fortresses had protected their occupants fully against the 16-inch naval shells. Until the shelling began, the Japanese staff and soldiers had not been sure whether their caves would really protect them.[3]

The American Landings

At 0830 on 1 April 1945, U.S. forces began to land on the Hagushi beaches (see map 4). The 32d Army believed there was a fifty-fifty chance that the Americans would land there rather than at Itoman or Minatoga. The Japanese believed the Americans would land in one place, or two at the most, since that had been their practice in the past. According to their established plan, the Japanese refrained both from firing artillery on the American beachhead and from responding to reconnaissance activities. The Americans did not expect such passivity since, even at Iwo Jima, the Japanese had directed artillery fires against the beaches.[4]

The main units of 32d Army did not stir from their underground positions in the south. Meeting the Americans around the Yontan and Kadena airfields, however, was the IJA 1st Specially Established Regiment, a unit that had only recently been formed out of the 56th and 44th Air Base Battalions and had little combat training. The Americans captured both airfields on the first day, a disappointment to the 32d Army Staff. The 1st Specially Established Regiment suffered heavy losses and retreated to the north, where it merged with the Kunigami Detachment, under whose command it had been placed on 2 April.[5]

The 32d Army had left no forces to the north of the Hagushi beaches except for this same Kunigami Detachment, whose orders were to delay the

Map 4. Movement of U.S. forces, 1—8 April 1945

U.S. forces on Hagushi beachhead on L+3

American advance while falling back northward. A Japanese detachment was a task-organized force of less than brigade size assembled for a particular combat mission and usually named for its commander, though here named for a place (north Okinawa). A detachment was usually organized around two or more regiments, a single regiment, or a battalion. The Japanese also used permanent task-organized brigades and regiments, with organic artillery, transport, signals, and such, which were then referred to as "independent mixed brigades" and "independent mixed regiments." The Kunigami Detachment in northern Okinawa consisted of the 44th IMB's 2d Infantry Regiment less its 3d Battalion, a force of about 1,715 men (see figure 3 in chapter 1).[6]

With Americans on the Hagushi beaches and expanding easily to the north and south, the 32d Army Staff formulated a series of attacks to push them back but then curiously abandoned or limited each as soon as it was made. The 10th Area Army on Taiwan and IGHQ in Tokyo pressured 32d Army to attack and recapture the Yontan and Kadena airfields. (IGHQ communicated with 32d Army by radio telegraphy.) This advice was almost redundant, however, since attack as a battle tactic was the predominant feature of Japanese infantry doctrine. Aggressive attack was supposed to catch the enemy off guard and force an early solution. Night infiltration and close combat were supposed to offset the enemy's advantage in firepower. Attack would overcome all problems, so elements of the 32d Army Staff, echoing IGHQ's wishes, repeatedly advocated attacking American lines in the early days of April.

Having been encouraged by a radio message from the 10th Area Army to attack and fearing harm to Commander Ushijima's reputation if an attack was not made, Chief of Staff Cho called a staff conference on the night of 3 April. He said the U.S. position was still in flux. Therefore, to annihilate this enemy, 32d Army should make a general attack immediately, relying on night infiltration and close combat, the form of fighting the IJA believed favored itself.[7]

Cho then canvassed the six staff members one by one to see if they agreed. The twelve staff men, Kumura, Jin, and the rest were junior to Cho in rank and age, being only majors and lieutenant colonels and eight to twenty years younger. These younger officers one by one enthusiastically agreed with Cho's suggestion, since it represented rock-solid IJA doctrine and since their superior was cuing them to this response. Major Jin Naomichi approved of the plan even more emphatically than the others because he was the aviation staff officer and so was eager to retake the airfields because of their importance for IGHQ's larger air and sea strategy. Only Major Nagano Hideo, an assistant strategy officer, qualified his approval somewhat.[8]

But in this atmosphere of total agreement, Operations Officer Yahara exploded against the attack policy. He spoke with the intensity of a man who knew he was right. He said that the young staff officers were agreeing to Cho's suggestions in an offhand manner, as if it were just a five-minute problem on an academy exam. He said they knew nothing of the terrain or other particular factors affecting the attack, even though this data was critical and actually had been gathered by Cho's subordinates.

They were making policy randomly, Yahara said, abandoning the policy of attrition warfare that had been carefully developed since the preceding autumn. Moreover, if they thought the Americans would be caught unprepared, that was "a complete fantasy." The Americans were already established on the beachhead, projecting orderly assault lines north and south, and would be still better organized after the three days it would take the Japanese to prepare a large-scale attack. Moving in the open under American guns would be suicidal and wreck 32d Army in a few days, which would be especially sad given the long toil preparing the elaborate tunnel positions. Besides that, he suggested, the radioed order from 10th Area Army for attack was not completely explicit, leaving local commanders some latitude to disregard it if doing so was in the army's interest on account of local circumstances.[9]

Cho heard this urgent speech to the end, saying nothing. When Yahara had finished his plea, Cho rose to his feet nonetheless and deliberately announced that the consensus of the meeting was that the staff favored attack. He recessed the group for thirty minutes, after which all officers reconvened in Lieutenant General Ushijima's office in full uniform and battle ribbons, to hear their commander request an attack by the main body of the army on the Yontan and Kadena airfields. A general attack was now the army's intention, and an attack plan in six paragraphs was drafted.[10]

Yahara was highly distraught over this impending waste, not only of the 32d Army but also of the past eight months of his own labors. Yahara therefore sought to lobby the various division commanders when they were briefed on the attack orders on 4 April. He urged each of them to voice opposition to the plan and did persuade one of them. The orders, however, remained in force.[11]

The attack was not scheduled until 6 April, however, and on the night of 4 April an air unit reported to 32d Army that an American task force of three aircraft carriers and fifty transports and cargo vessels had been spotted ninety miles south of Naha. If the Americans landed at Machinato airfield, just behind the existing forward line, at the same moment as the Japanese attack, the result would be catastrophic. Yahara seized on this message and carried it to Cho, who summarily canceled the 6 April offensive that had caused the 32d Army Staff so much turmoil for the last several days.[12]

Although Yahara seemed to be a minority of one in the attack dispute, coolly discarding thirty years of IJA doctrine, it was nevertheless his point of view that prevailed in the end. The 6 April offensive was canceled and never took place. This first episode of nonattack was significant because most of 32d Army's decisions for the rest of its existence would be reached in this same stormy way: by a test of wills and words between Cho and Yahara.

The two men had different personalities. Cho was famous for physical courage, spontaneous decision, and a hearty presence that inspired confidence and friendship. Yahara was known as a sour, aloof, preoccupied intellectual. The disputes between them pitted romantic aspiration against reality and rosy doctrine against harsh fact. The most surprising feature of this turbulent decision-making process, however, was that most observers felt it produced good decisions.

Planning the Japanese 12 April Offensive

From the earliest days of the American presence up until the major Japanese offensive of 4 May, there was a continuing tendency in 32d Army to go over to the attack, with Yahara in every case trying to stem the tide. The attack impulse came from higher headquarters as well as from doctrinal habit, since the staffs of 10th Area Army on Taiwan and of IGHQ in Tokyo couched their expectations in terms of their strategic goals rather than in terms of the realities of the Okinawa field.

On the night of 5 April, when 10th Area Army heard that the 6 April offensive had been canceled, it immediately radioed that 32d Army must attack on the night of 8 April to recapture the airfields. This time the message was a specific command. Consequently, Lieutenant General Ushijima's response was to issue an order for a general attack for the night of 8 April, the order's text being similar to that of the just-canceled 6 April attack.[13]

Once again, however, on the afternoon of 7 April, an American naval group was observed moving west of Naha, causing fears of an American landing near Machinato and an advance toward Urasoe village, behind the left flank of the Japanese main line. Cho therefore modified the attack orders into only a night sortie by two companies in front of their positions, a gesture of little consequence.[14]

When no landings materialized, Cho instructed Yahara on 8 April to prepare a night attack for 12 April. A brigade or more would cross U.S. lines, and small units would penetrate deeply. If successful, a general attack would follow immediately. Two young staff officers, Kimura and Kusumaru, who had served in China, thought a night penetration of six miles was possible. Yahara thought it was the height of folly but prepared the plan in his usual businesslike way.[15]

The American Advance

Meanwhile, the Americans had moved four divisions onto the Hagushi beaches (see map 4). By 3 April they had secured most of the Hagushi landmass, and their southern perimeter crossed the isthmus at Futema. By 8 April, the Americans had pushed the Kunigami Detachment northward as far as the Motobu Peninsula and the Gaya Detachment southward back into the Japanese main line (the Gaya Detachment was a small force sent out, like its counterpart, the Kunigami, to delay the U.S. advance).[16]

The U.S. 1st and 6th Marine Divisions were able to secure all of Motobu Peninsula by 20 April, despite stubborn resistance by remnants of the Kunigami Detachment on Yae-Take Mountain. This meant that the two-thirds of Okinawa north of the Hagushi beachhead was all essentially pacified by that date. Only a few Kunigami troops remained in the hills until the end of the campaign. Meanwhile, from 16 to 22 April, the U.S. 77th Infantry Division was securing Ie Island from its defenders (part of the Kunigami Detachment).[17]

However, the Americans' easy advance toward the south ended on 8 April. The main struggle on Okinawa would take place on the southern isthmus where, on 8 April, the U.S. 7th and 96th Infantry Divisions were just pushing up against the main Japanese line for the first time. This arrival happened while the Japanese still debated whether to attack, and it had two important consequences for the Japanese operational situation. One was that the units of the IJA 62d Division that manned the main line were engaged and could not easily move for an attack. The other was that now it was not necessary to attack to achieve the close combat IJA favored, because the Americans had obligingly provided this circumstance by moving forward.

The Japanese 12 April Offensive

The U.S. 7th and 96th Infantry Divisions kept steady pressure on the Japanese isthmus line from 9 April on, while preparing for a major offensive thrust that would begin on 19 April. At the 32d Army Staff headquarters, the plans for the Japanese 12 April attacks went forward. The units of the IJA 62d Division already on the isthmus line were to hold. The IJA 22d Infantry Regiment was to be brought north from the Oroku area, placed under 62d Division's command, and assembled northeast of Shuri. At sunset, the 22d was to attack through the U.S. lines on the east of the Ginowan Road, then advance as far as Shimabuku (see map 5).[18]

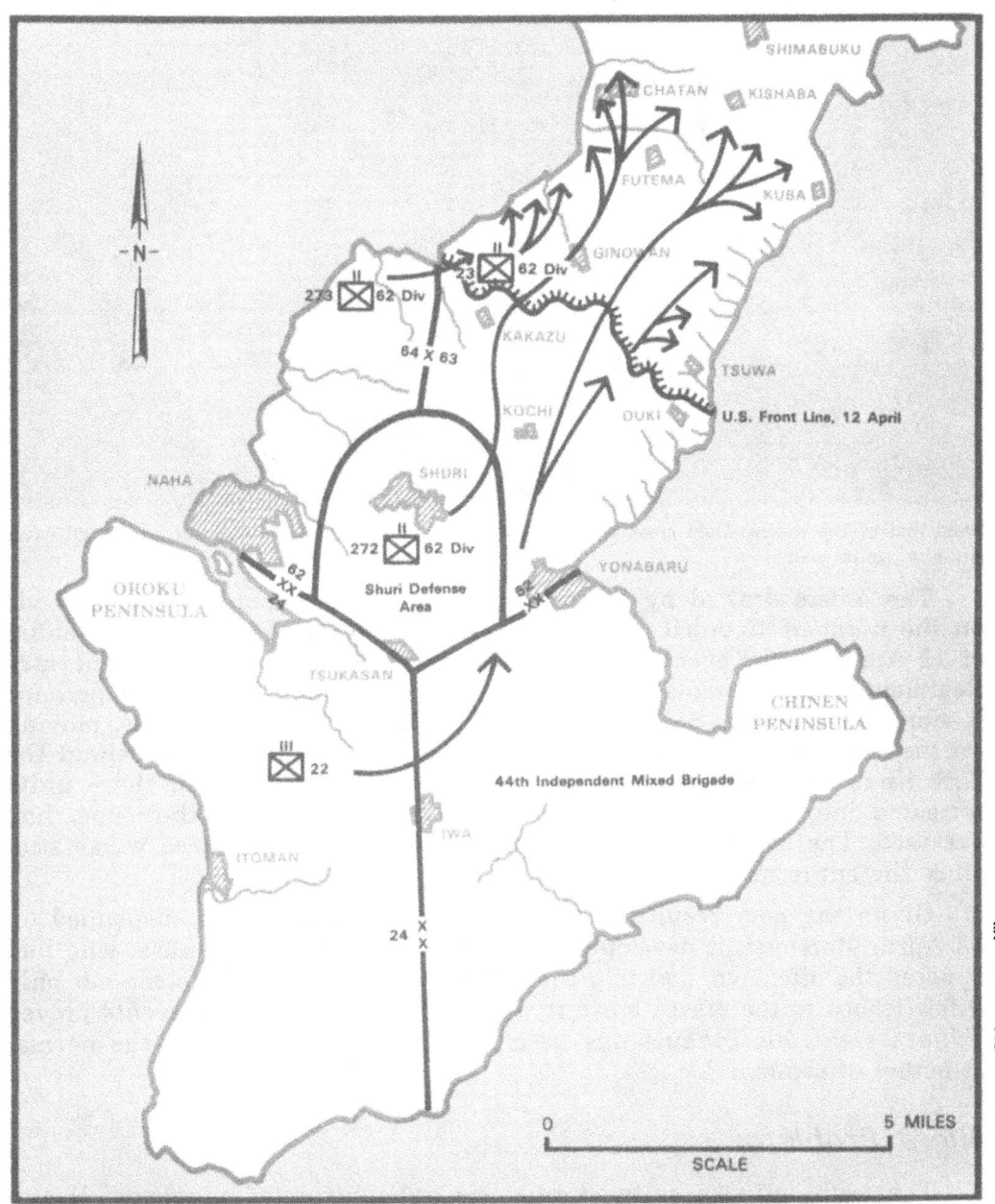

Map 5. Plan for the IJA's 12 April offensive

The 62d Division was to use three reserve battalions from its own rear areas—the 23d, 272d, and 273d—for the sunset assault. The 273d Battalion was to attack along the west coast, the 272d was to advance along the west side of the Ginowan Road, and the 23d was to move forward between them. The 32d Army artillery was to provide covering fire beginning at sunset, with fires briefly directed at the American line, then shifted to American rear areas.[19]

West end of the Kakazu-Ouki crest line that was fortified by IJA 32d Army across the Okinawa isthmus' whole width

The orders drafted by Yahara were handed to subordinate commands on the night of 10 April and were carried out on schedule on the evening of 12 April. In the event, the rightmost assault unit, the IJA 22d Infantry Regiment, failed to move forward because of unfamiliar terrain or perhaps it simply got lost in the darkness.[20] The 23d and 272d Battalions, moving on the west side of the Ginowan Road, penetrated 1,000 yards behind the U.S. lines but were isolated after dawn on 13 April. When these units retreated into the Japanese lines that night, only half of their men had survived. The 273d Battalion, moving up the west coast, fared worse still, since the entire unit was lost.[21]

Given the poor results, Ushijima ordered the offensive suspended on 13 April. Moreover, it developed that Senior Staff Officer Yahara, who had opposed the offensive, had told the 62d Division commander to commit only a few troops to the attack since it was bound to fail. Though events proved Yahara right, his conduct has been criticized as undermining the normal structure of command.[22]

Night Problems

The night attacks suffered from several unexpected problems. Heavy shelling had changed the landscape, blasting away villages and thickets, so that even though night infiltrators knew their maps and thought they knew the terrain, they lacked the landmarks needed to tell them where they actually were. Moreover, frequent illumination shells forced the eyes of night infiltrators to adjust so many times that their capacity to adjust was lost. They became temporarily blinded and so were unable to move.[23]

Because of the unfamiliar terrain and flash blindness, the Japanese night fighters had difficulty reaching their assigned objectives. In fact, it was hard for them to reach their jumping-off points. Continuous naval bombardment of crossroads and bridges forced units to rush across in small groups between shells so that the units became strung out on the roads and difficult to control. It was hard to move heavy ammunition and supplies forward because of these interdiction points and the generally churned up roads. Even when units reached their northward assembly points safely by night, they were immediately exposed to aerial observation and artillery fire at dawn, since they lacked enough time to dig in. Units that attacked across American lines safely in darkness had the same problem: they lacked time to dig in and so were utterly exposed to artillery fire at morning light. Night attacks, like flanking maneuver, were a kind of cure-all in prewar Japanese doctrine. But they failed to provide the expeditious results on Okinawa that IJA doctrine had led the 32d Army Staff to expect.[24]

Moving the Army North

On 19 April, U.S. Army's XXIV Corps launched the major offensive it had been preparing for ten days along the whole Kakazu-Ouki line (see map 6). The IJA 62d Division, which held this line and had suffered in the 12 April attacks, was becoming increasingly weakened, to the point where the whole 32d Army Staff agreed it would soon collapse. The 62d Division had already been ordered, after the 12 April offensive, to put its reserve units on the line so that each of the 62d's thinned battalions could shorten its front. By 19 April, the 62d Division had lost 35 percent of its personnel and 39 percent of its artillery.[25]

After four days of the new American offensive, 62d Division still held firm but had been pushed back one-half mile from its 19 April positions. In hard fighting it had relinquished Nishibaru Ridge in the center and the neighboring ridges on its right. The 62d Division was most undermined, however, by the U.S. 27th Infantry Division's penetration on the Japanese left. By aggressive and persistent advances, the 27th had thrust a salient into the Japanese line just east of Gusukuma village, thus isolating the Japanese forces on the western coastal heights from the rest of the Japanese line.[26]

By 22 April, the IJA 62d Division had lost half of its original strength and was nearly broken through on the left. Operations Officer Yahara was in a quandary over this. He estimated that for every battalion, field gun, and mortar the 62d Division had on the line, the U.S. XXIV Corps had 4, not to mention the 100 tanks and 640 aircraft Yahara calculated to be at XXIV Corps' disposal.[27]

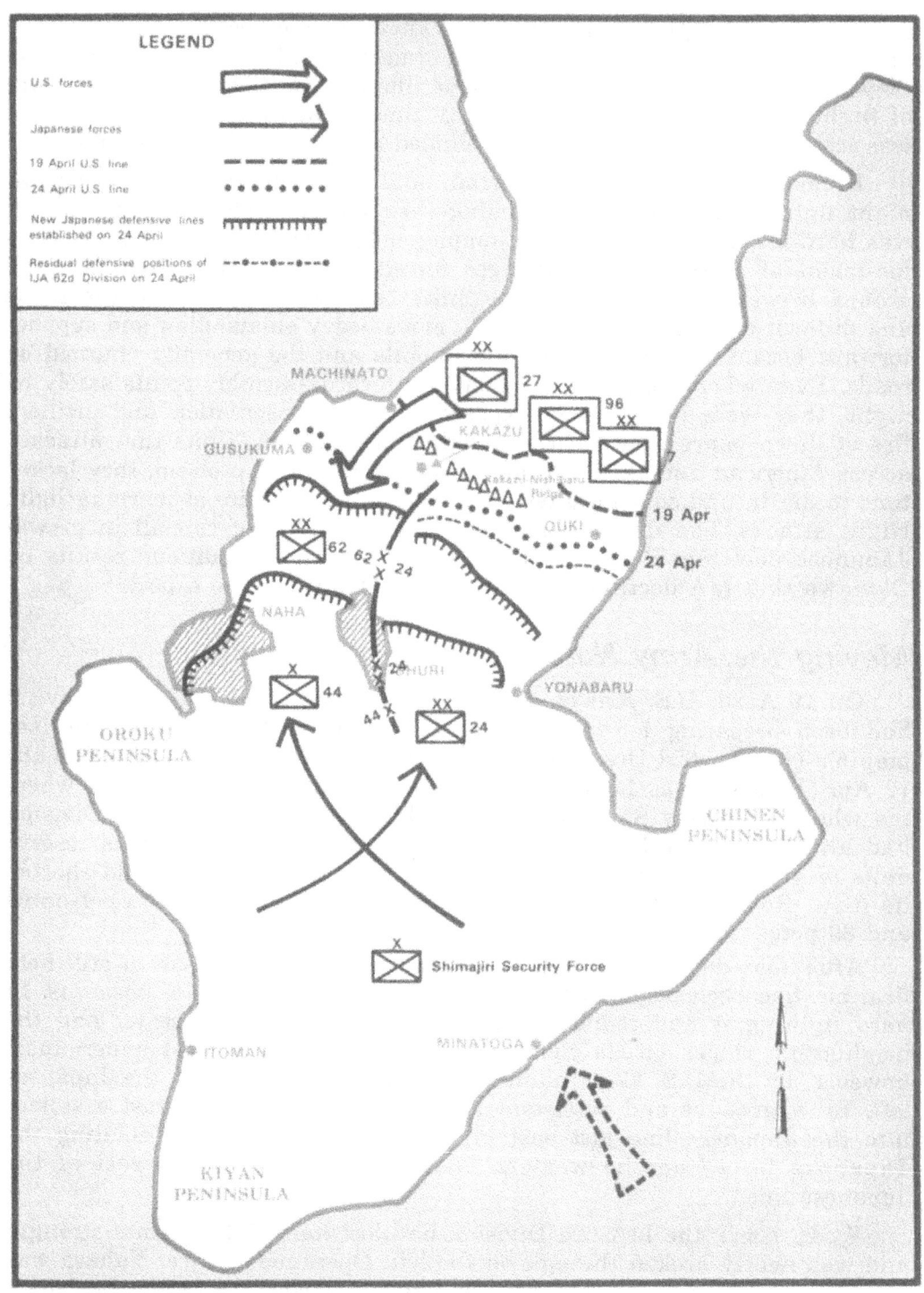

Map 6. The IJA positions as of 25 April 1945

Eastern portion of the Kakazu-Ouki crest line. IJA forces lost this strong defensive position in heavy fighting after 19 April and tried to restore it on 4 May.

Americans approaching the Nishibaru Ridge in the center of the IJA Kakazu-Ouki line, still intact as of 19 April

In pondering the Americans' next move, however—Yahara's constant preoccupation—he judged that the U.S. Tenth Army had six divisions ashore, of which only the 27th, 96th, and 7th Infantry Divisions were deployed on the Kakazu-Ouki line. As he considered the operational facts from the American viewpoint, Yahara was convinced that it was in the Americans' best interest to use amphibious envelopment and land a force of a division or more on Okinawa's southeast coast at Minatoga. This would force Japanese combat units to fight on two fronts and could lead to an early collapse of the overextended Japanese perimeter. The U.S. Tenth Army did, in fact, send escorted transports to the Minatoga coast on 19 April to threaten a landing.[28]

For the IJA 24th Division to be facing the southwest coast and the 44th IMB to be facing the southeast coast was an ideal arrangement to counter a second American front, but they could not be left there because the Japanese 62d Division line in the north was itself about to disintegrate. So Yahara developed two alternatives to the present Japanese dispositions. One was to move the 24th Division and 44th IMB to the north to reinforce the 62d Division line. The other alternative was to abandon the northern line and draw the 32d Army into three strongpoints in the Shuri, Kiyan, and Chinen areas. Both approaches would shorten the perimeter being defended.[29]

Yahara felt on the whole that moving the bulk of IJA forces to the northern line was the sounder course, but he was dismayed still by the prospect of an American landing in the rear. He was so uncertain that he took all of these problems to Lieutenant General Cho on 22 April and asked him what to do. It is a measure of his consternation that this was the only time he ever consulted Cho about operations.[30]

Cho said without hesitation that the 32d Army would be lost if the 62d Division were not reinforced immediately. So 24th Division and 44th IMB must be moved north for that purpose. If the Americans landed in the south, the Japanese would address that when it happened. "A man who chases two rabbits won't catch either one," he added, quoting the Japanese proverb. Cho's decision was quick and clear, which made moving the troops north seem to be obviously the right course. Cho had a decisive confidence and radiated this to the staff around him. His cutting the knot put Yahara's tormented mind at ease. To reach the right answers quickly without worrying about them too much was Cho's forte. Yahara was grateful.[31]

Since the IJA 62d Division line was so badly pocked, Yahara decided to use only part of the reinforcements, elements of the IJA 24th Division, to take over the right half of the 62d Division's line, while using the rest of the reinforcements to form a solid, fresh defense line a mile to the rear. The 24th Division was to hold the line from Shuri eastward and the 44th IMB was to hold it from Shuri westward, deploying behind the 62d Division. This would allow defense of the forward line to be continuous and, at the same time, provide a still unencroached defensive position in the rear into which retreating forces could fall back gradually. The southern areas would be manned only by a so-called Shimajiri Security Force of 5,500 men, created out of rear-area supply units. Its job was to delay any American thrust from the south until main-force units could return to the area.[32]

By the night of 24 April, the 24th Division and the 44th IMB had moved into their new northern positions. The American forces were completely unaware of the concealed night movements of these units. In the next few days, however, Japanese soldiers on the line were seen with 24th Division markings, revealing to the Americans that at least some of the IJA 24th Division had moved up from the south. For the Americans, IJA operations on the northern line were only too continuous. They remained unaware that the Japanese had faced a grave operational dilemma. To U.S. Tenth Army, the only visible phenomenon was the constant, smooth functioning of the resistance line in front of them.[33]

Even so, the U.S. Tenth Army actually was considering whether to land on the Minatoga coast at almost the same moment Yahara was agonizing over that possibility. The idea was advanced not by the U.S. Tenth Army staff but by field commanders of the still unengaged units. Major General Andrew Bruce, commander of the U.S. 77th Infantry Division, urged as the Ie Island fighting was ending that his division be landed on the Minatoga beaches, behind the Japanese main line, rather than merely being fed on line in the north. The 77th Infantry Division had had success with such a maneuver on Leyte when it landed at Ormoc behind Japanese lines. (Yahara was also nervously aware of the recent Leyte precedent.)

Lieutenant General Simon Bolivar Buckner and the U.S. Tenth Army staff rejected Bruce's request, however, on the grounds that the Minatoga beaches were too constricted to stage provisions and ordnance adequately, even for a single division. The steep terrain near the beaches favored the defense, and any unit there would be isolated. It might be more like Anzio than Leyte, he suggested. Besides that, the three divisions on the line needed to be relieved, and Buckner's three unused divisions would all be needed there.[34] When it was determined about 26 April that the entire IJA 24th Division was on the northern line, Major General John R. Hodge, commander of XXIV Corps, went to the U.S. Tenth Army staff and advocated a landing at Minatoga, as Major General Bruce had, since Japanese defenses there were thin. The Tenth Army staff officers again rejected the proposal, just as Buckner had a few days before, and for similar reasons.[35]

Buckner's decision not to open a second front in the south was, and remains, controversial. It is still not clear whether a division landed at Minatoga would have caused the Japanese perimeter to collapse early, or merely have caused the gradual attrition phenomenon to take place on a different terrain, or even have resulted in a U.S. division's being pinned down on a hostile beach. The workaday calculations of the Tenth Army staff may have been correct. The Japanese forces, even at the end of May, were still able to move the six miles between northern and southern fronts unobserved and within a few days. The U.S. forces at Minatoga would have had no developed rear areas to draw on and would soon have faced defense caves reoccupied by the IJA 24th Division. The IJA 5th Artillery Command, placed on interior lines, could have brought its full weight to bear on Minatoga without moving away from the northern front. But the U.S. XXIV Corps artillery, located north of the Shuri line, could not have reached Minatoga to cover a U.S. division there (though abundant naval artillery could have been used). All in all, Buckner's judgment may have been right.

Yahara had trouble anticipating Buckner's decision because of two considerations that loomed large for Buckner but not for Yahara. One was that Buckner's staff members had a practical sense of the terrain needed to support the Americans' high-volume logistics so that they, but not Yahara, could see those conditions did not exist at Minatoga. The other factor was that Buckner was aware of how worn American line units were becoming in continuous combat on the isthmus line, something that had not occurred to Yahara.

Lethality in Motion: Tactics

The fighting on Okinawa had features that were all its own, but even so its dynamics bore a startling resemblance to the fierce no-man's-land fighting of World War I. The conditions of warfare for both sides, but especially for the Japanese, were governed by the reality of the caves. The Okinawa caves were in some ways a unique response to the lethal mass of enemy artillery the IJA 32d Army faced, and given what they were intended to do, the caves were extremely successful.

Cave Warfare

The caves were largely responsible for the denseness and immobility of the fighting on Okinawa. Without them the Japanese would not have been able to continue to fight at all, and they greatly influenced the tactics both sides found themselves using. As an operational device, the Okinawa caves surpassed the trench systems of World War I in some respects, and in their self-sufficiency the caves were an evolution toward the style of tunnel system used by the North Vietnamese at Cu Chi.

The Command Cave

The most elaborate of the caves was the headquarters structure for the IJA 32d Army, far below Shuri Castle (see figure 4). The headquarters tunnel ran 1,280 feet north to south, with side chambers and a side shaft angling to the left at the north end. The 5th Artillery Command had its tunnel, about 200 yards long, just to the west. The 62d Division headquarters cave lay 300 yards to the east.[1]

The 32d Army's command cave lay under sloping terrain, beneath 160 feet of earth at its deepest point, and beneath 50 to 100 feet for most of its length. The 32d's command functions were all placed in sixty yards of the northwestern extremity of the tunnel's side shaft. The commanders were fortunate to be below Shuri Castle rather than in it because as the battle progressed its handsome buildings and parks were reduced to a rubbled moonscape.[2]

Unlike the smaller frontline caves, the headquarters cave had all walls faced with sawed planks and supported with squared beams. Access shafts

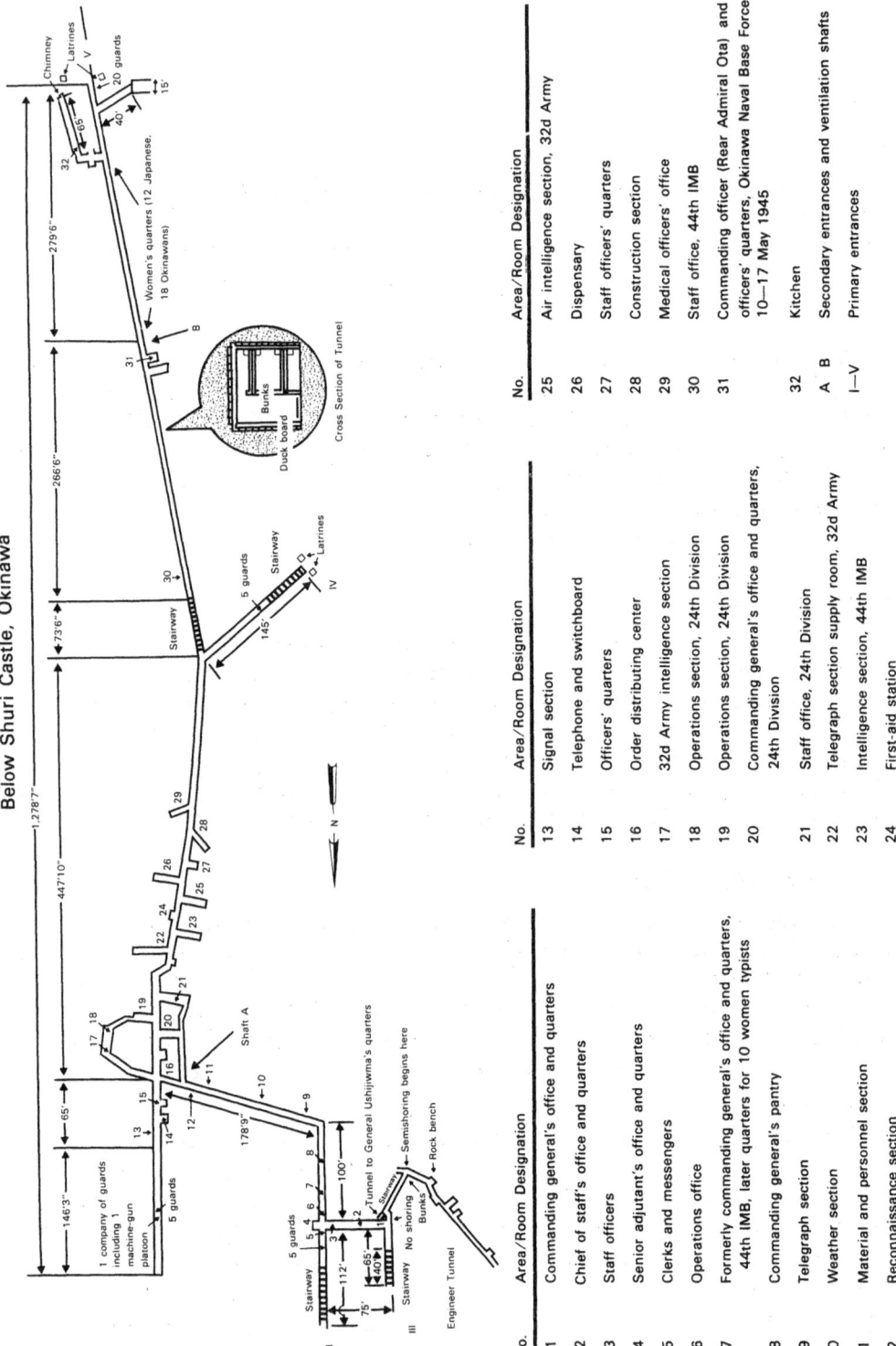

Floor Plan of the Japanese 32d Army Headquarters Below Shuri Castle, Okinawa

No.	Area/Room Designation
1	Commanding general's office and quarters
2	Chief of staff's office and quarters
3	Staff officers
4	Senior adjutant's office and quarters
5	Clerks and messengers
6	Operations office
7	Formerly commanding general's office and quarters, 44th IMB, later quarters for 10 women typists
8	Commanding general's pantry
9	Telegraph section
10	Weather section
11	Material and personnel section
12	Reconnaissance section

No.	Area/Room Designation
13	Signal section
14	Telephone and switchboard
15	Officers' quarters
16	Order distributing center
17	32d Army intelligence section
18	Operations section, 24th Division
19	Operations section, 24th Division
20	Commanding general's office and quarters, 24th Division
21	Staff office, 24th Division
22	Telegraph section supply room, 32d Army
23	Intelligence section, 44th IMB
24	First-aid station

No.	Area/Room Designation
25	Air intelligence section, 32d Army
26	Dispensary
27	Staff officers' quarters
28	Construction section
29	Medical officers' office
30	Staff office, 44th IMB
31	Commanding officer (Rear Admiral Ota) and officers' quarters, Okinawa Naval Base Force, 10—17 May 1945
32	Kitchen
A B	Secondary entrances and ventilation shafts
I—V	Primary entrances

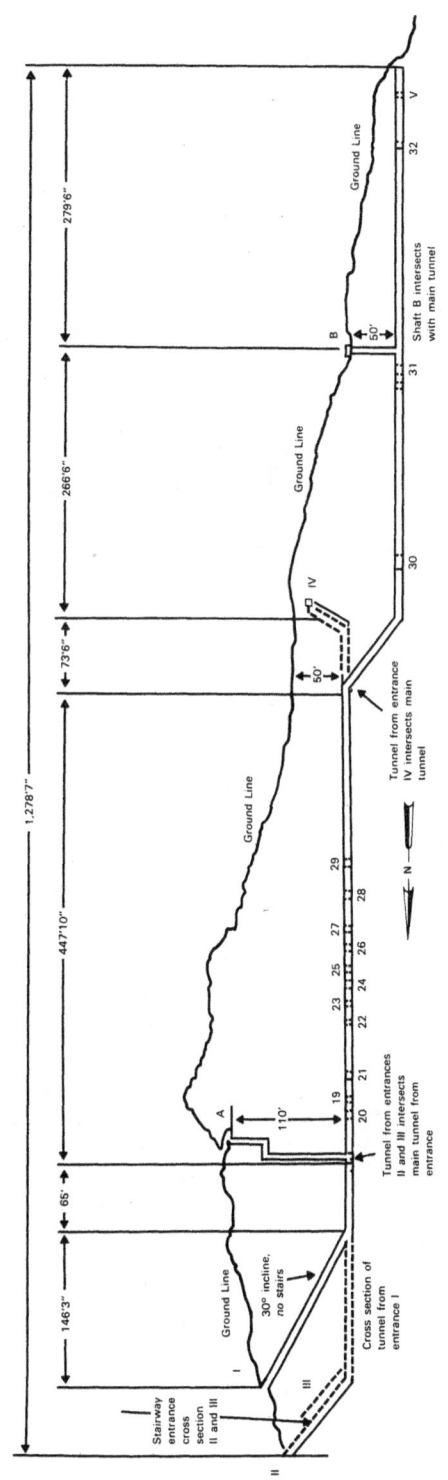

Figure 4. The Shuri command cave

Shuri Castle before and after the Okinawa battle

One of the vertical shafts that allowed access to the Shuri headquarters cave

Headquarters cave office still showing a semblance of order despite demolition efforts by withdrawing Japanese

Motor that ran headquarters cave ventilator fan

were provided with wooden ladders and landings every four yards or so. Climbing straight up 50 to 100 feet in these shafts was arduous. The furnishings were simple but useful, rather like an IJA barracks. Offices were set up with desks and chairs and had electricity. The commander's pantry was notoriously well stocked, and seventy-two feet of tunnel at the south end served as the headquarters kitchen. Elaborate measures were taken to lead the smoke outlets to points where they would be screened from the Americans' view. In the soldiers' areas, bunks ran lengthwise along the side of the tunnel. The functions and spaces of the tunnels took on the quality of a warship.[3]

As far as enemy fire was concerned, the Shuri command tunnel was completely safe. Life there, however, was not without its hardships. According to Yahara, the atmosphere was hot and humid—over 90 degrees Fahrenheit with 100 percent humidity. Walls sweated and desks and chairs were sticky with moisture. The inhabitants developed skin rashes because their skin never dried. A large ventilator fan placed in one of the access shafts to bring in fresh air had a limited effect. Moreover, rice stored in the tunnels began to ferment in the sack, giving it a sour taste when served. Besides that, given the command staff, the sentries, the numerous messengers, and the headquarters company, there were over 1,000 troops in the tunnel. This made the air not only stuffy but also filled with human aromas. The press of people itself was a kind of hardship.[4]

On the other hand, boosting morale, thirty bright young women did office work in the cave, twelve Japanese and eighteen Okinawan, and had their own living quarters at the cave's south end. There were also some creature comforts. Staples and canned goods were stored in abundance, and tasty dinners were provided for the staff by the chef Chief of Staff Cho had brought from Fukuoka. Cho had also brought a pastry chef, who prepared the refreshments for afternoon tea. Fresh vegetables were harder to come by, but the sentries outside managed to forage some tomatoes and Chinese cabbage from neighboring gardens. Beer and sake were plentiful, and the commander's cabinet held respectable Scotch whiskeys. Though cigarettes soon grew moldy in the dampness of the cave, lucky staff members occasionally could get fresh Camels, as Yahara did, from miscarried American parachute drops.[5]

Besides the physical rigors, there were psychological pressures that accompanied cave life. The headquarters cave was a "nightless palace" where electric lights burned day and night, which was disorienting. Since messengers could move only at night,* the battle situation could not begin to be pieced together until well after dark. The situation then had to be analyzed, a response determined, and orders drafted. The result was to reverse night and day for the staff, which could not complete its work until just before dawn. Yahara wrote afterwards that he would fall asleep at dawn just as the American bombardment was beginning, with "the feeling he was being dragged to the bottom of hell." The strange life of the caves, even though shielded from battle, took its toll. Even the formidable Cho began mumbling in his sleep, "Mother, it hurts."[6]

Line and Artillery Caves

Although the 32d Army headquarters tunnel was the most imposing of the caves, there were many other underground structures, enough to house all 100,000 men of 32d Army underground, 60 miles of tunnels in all. These caves were all located at the south end of Okinawa in an area three to twelve miles wide and sixteen miles long: the whole battle area was honey-

---

*Communication below battalion level was by messenger. Communication at battalion level and above was by field telephone, but artillery bombardment often cut the telephone lines. Thus communication even at battalion level and above was often by messenger. See 10th Army, *Monograph*, pt. I, sect. D, chap. IV, p. 1.

combed with defensive fortifications. Each unit at company and battalion level was responsible for building its own tunnels. This seemed to guarantee that the job was done thoroughly but also meant that there was considerable variety in the tunnel patterns. It meant further that fire nets were not well integrated for units larger than battalion.[7]

There was enough variety in the construction of the caves that one American officer described them as "artful and fantastic." Even so, what mainly varied was size, function, and the degree to which they were finished. The headquarters caves were the most elaborate. At the other extreme were the supply caves designed to hold ammunition and food. These differed from other tunnels in that they had wide mouths, wide shafts, and large chambers and did not have multiple openings. They were just modest underground storage rooms. One example of this type was found by Americans near the north end of the Okinawa isthmus (see figure 5).[8] Somewhat akin to this style was the underground barracks room. This type featured long underground shafts with one or several entrances, a vertical air duct, a chamber fifteen feet by fifteen feet by six feet for dining, and another chamber for sleeping. Like the storerooms, these underground barracks were not fortifications.[9]

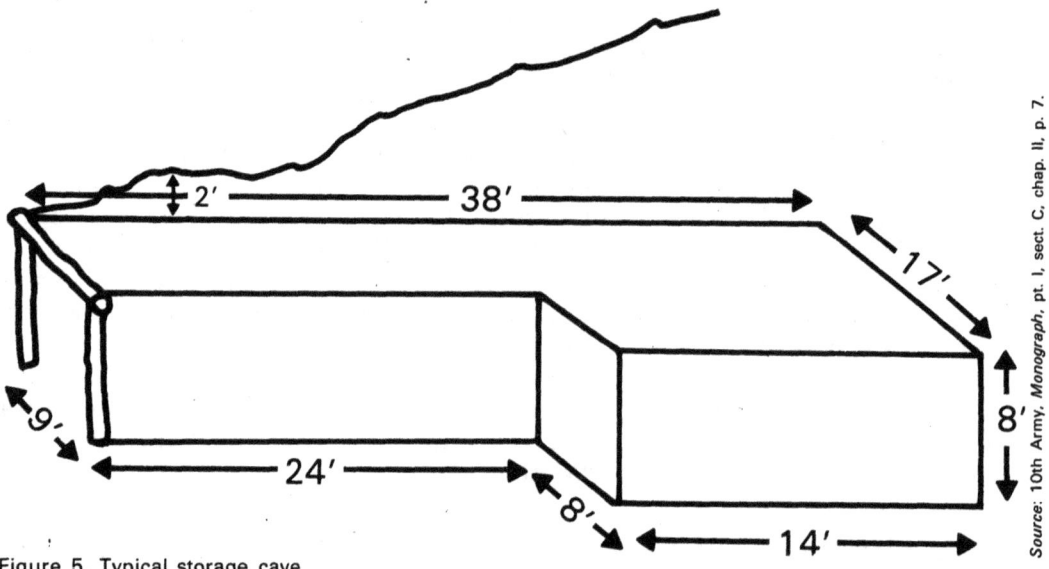

Figure 5. Typical storage cave

Most of the honeycomb of tunnels the Japanese companies and battalions built for themselves, however, were underground fighting positions. Although these forts were made in a great variety of sizes and patterns, the principles they followed were all remarkably the same: they were pillboxes (see figure 6). The cave pillbox positions were in a sense not underground. Because of the undulating terrain and because the Japanese used only reverse-slope tactics, their technique was to dig horizontal shafts into the hill or ridge opposite the one they intended to cover with fire. Therefore,

A storage cave entryway

A storage cave interior

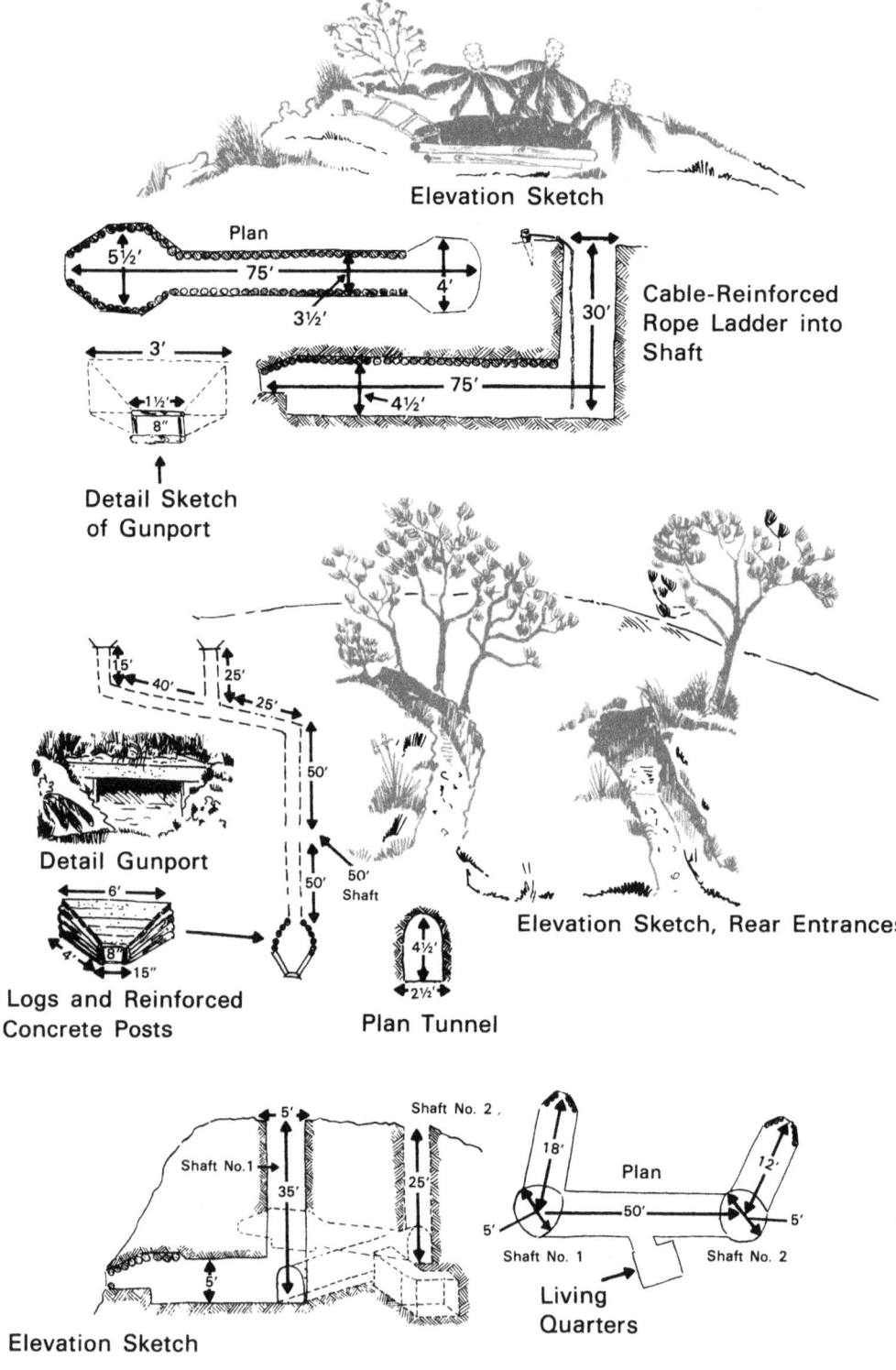

Figure 6. Typical pillbox caves

when they looked out their fire ports, their perspective was one of a person at ground level or above. The caves' entrances were made by extending the cave shaft to the rear of the same hill whose front slope had the fire port. One entered the tunnel from the rear, without descending. These so-called caves might also be described as hilltop fortresses since they offered complete protection while also commanding the terrain. This may have kept the Japanese inhabitants' morale higher than that of their counterparts in World War I trenches or the caves of Cu Chi.

Inconspicuous vertical entrance of the upper example of line cave represented in figure 6

There was variety in the pillbox patterns due both to how many men were available in an area to labor on a cave (and then dwell in it) and to what terrain features were available. Sometimes a whole round hilltop would be taken over with fire ports pierced out of every side and multiple concealed entrances on the side the enemy was least likely to approach. The air ventilation shaft would be extended vertically.[10]

More often defenders found themselves on a continuous ridge that, unlike the round-topped hills, did not offer the possibility of side shafts, so shafts were cut straight back from the fire position. In the most elementary and most common of these, a shaft four and a half feet high and three and a half feet wide (as opposed to five feet by six feet in the deluxe Shuri headquarters cave) was pushed far back into the hillside, with a vertical entry shaft only if the back side of the hill was too far away. If there was a vertical entry shaft, it would have a simple rope and bamboo ladder, and its mouth would be covered by a wooden lid crafted like part of a traditional

52

Fire port of the type of line cave represented in figure 6. The hard-to-see opening is indicated by a broken white line.

Coopered lid for pillbox cave entrance

Lids covered with sod became nearly invisible

Wooden beams supported earthen shafts

Vertical shaft of pillbox cave

Stone shaft of a pillbox cave

56

Wooden beams supported earthen shafts

Underground mess hall on Oroku Peninsula

Commander's office in a pillbox cave complex

Caves were linked by communications trenches

Communications trench with bamboo arches for overhead camouflage

Japanese barrel and camouflaged with sod. The firing room was widened to perhaps five and a half feet, then tapered to the fire port. The port itself might be as small as eight inches wide, with earth splayed outward from that opening to a width of three feet. This made it easy to fire out and hard to fire in. Just inside the port was a dais, a foot or so above the floor, on which was placed a machine gun or other fire weapon.[11] All the construction in such a position consisted of shaped earth, with hand-cut logs to shore up the walls and the external splaying. The few men who manned the position usually lived inside in a slightly widened chamber or side shaft.[12]

Since responsibility for building the caves lay with the battalions, communications between caves, like the fire nets between them, were well integrated at battalion level and below, but not above. Nearby caves were sometimes linked by tunnel. Caves farther apart were linked by communications trenches so soldiers could go between them unseen. The larger caves had multiple entrances, and entrances in general, like the fire ports, were small and artfully concealed.[13]

American observers felt that, "in some of the larger hill masses," extensive tunnels provided "underground mobility" to the Japanese that allowed them to "convert an apparent defensive operation into an offensive one by moving [their] troops through tunnels into different . . . pillboxes."[14] Some of the through-the-hill cave systems did allow the Japanese free movement all around a terrain feature without being seen.

Even so, the IJA 32d Army Staff was impressed with the extent to which being fixed in the caves limited 32d Army's mobility. Because the building of communications trenches had not been coordinated above battalion level, it was not impossible for large forces to maneuver out of sight. Even if they did manage to move, there was often no room for them in the already inhabited caves where they arrived. When preparing for attack, the problem could be overcome by painstakingly moving forces at night. But when responding to U.S. attacks, which always came in the day, large forces could not be moved from one network of underground positions to another. Concentrating forces to resist an attack or mount a counterattack was impossible.[15]

This meant that Japanese soldiers in an attacked position had to defend to the death, because their comrades could not come forward to aid them, nor for that matter, could they retreat in the open without being exposed to massive American fire.[16] The cave forts, although they protected the IJA force, sharply reduced its mobility, and agility was out of the question. This problem could have been partially overcome if the Japanese had paid more attention to building communications trenches between the scores of small cave systems.

American officers reported that the Japanese used the caves to maneuver behind the U.S. lines.[17] But it is more likely that the Japanese were trapped in their caves behind the Americans as a consequence of the Americans' forward movement. The cave positions prevented out-of-sight rearward mobility. Because the Japanese could not safely retreat, some ended up behind the American lines, though neither they nor the Americans wished for them to be there.

Fire port of a 150-mm naval gun position

While the whole Japanese infantry was installed in pillbox caves, so was its artillery—large guns and small. Although the size of the cave varied according to the size of the gun, the configuration and function of the artillery caves were essentially the same as those of the infantry machine-gun caves. One of the two 150-mm naval guns overlooking Nakagusuku (Buckner) Bay, for example, was set in a concrete-walled room twenty-five feet by fifteen feet, with a reinforced concrete fire port eight feet wide. The gun crew lived in a long shaft behind the firing room. In short the big-gun forts, like the machine-gun forts, were just fire slots with tunnel shelters behind them (see figure 7).[18]

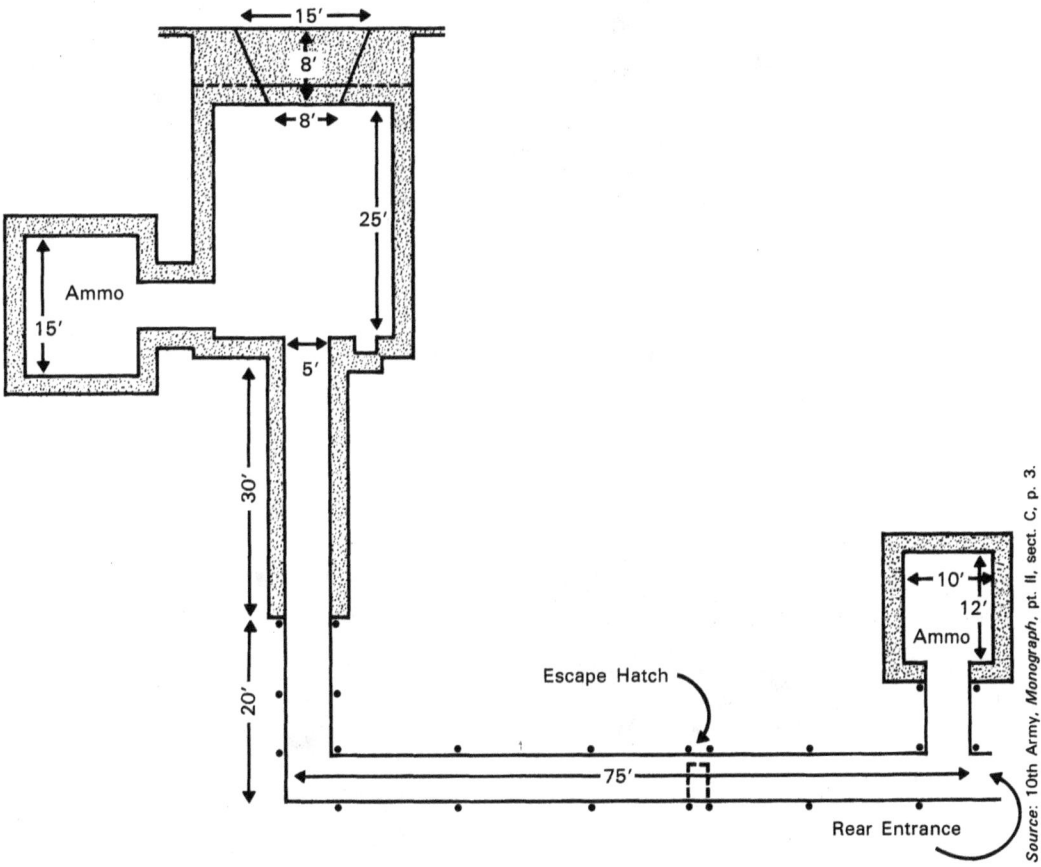

Figure 7. An IJN 150-mm naval gun position

Searchlights and naval range finders were set next to a line-of-sight opening with a barracks tunnel behind, just as the guns were. In other words, the "window-on-the-world" approach was adopted for all line-of-sight related functions. A semicircular variation was provided for mortars. Typically, a ten-foot semicircular room was set four and a half feet into the ground with a fan-shaped, hardened, camouflaged roof at ground level and an underground shaft running behind. Fire slots were created at intervals along the 180 degrees around the edge of the roof by removing some of the ground (see figure 8).[19]

Rear wall of the fire room of a 150-mm naval gun position

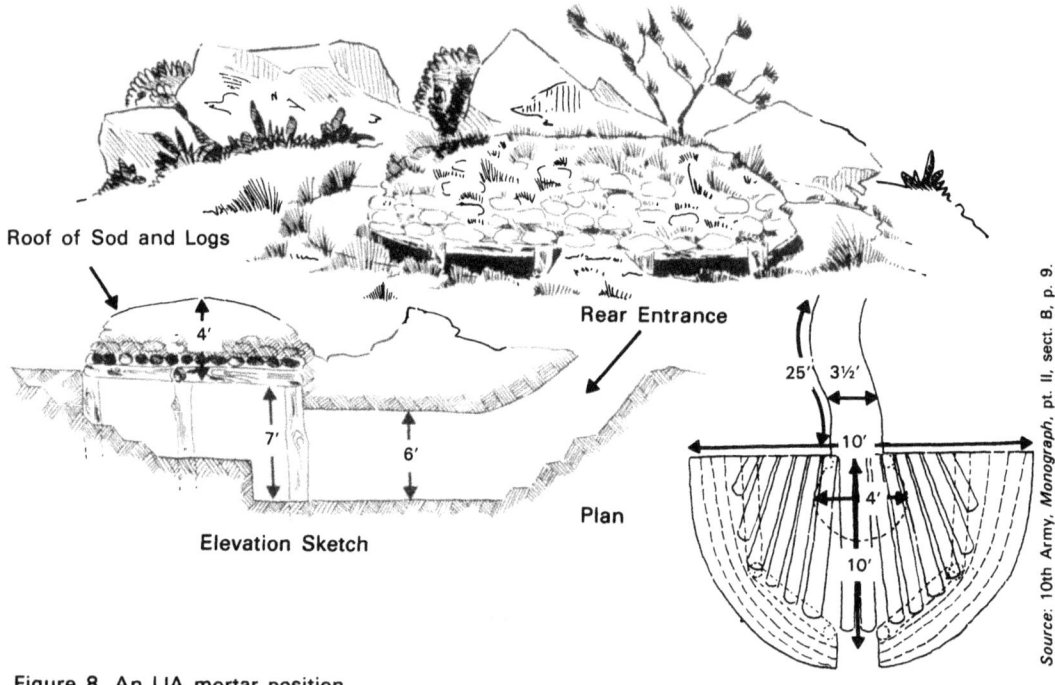

Figure 8. An IJA mortar position

Mortar position fire port

Cave Warfare: Some Comparisons

There were several factors that made the cave positions on Okinawa different from the trench systems of World War I. On Okinawa both sides knew well in advance where the battle would be. Both knew also that, although one side would have overwhelming firepower and air supremacy, the other side would have exclusive control of the ground for a year before combat. American air supremacy meant that every Japanese position had to be hardened and concealed, because air observation would bring devastating bombardment on any visible target. The Japanese' long foreknowledge of the inevitable attack, coupled with their unlimited labor power, meant that the Japanese could respond to this problem with an elaborate solution: moving everything underground. The Americans, similarly, were hindered by having no access to the ground.

The IJA, relying on its only advantage—prior access—managed largely to neutralize the American triple threat of air, naval, and field artillery bombardment through eleven weeks of combat. Even so, since the caves were built without the Japanese knowing exactly where the Americans would land, they were not concentrated where the front would be, not well fire-integrated above battalion level, and not well connected for movement. The World War I trench systems avoided all these defects because of the doubtful advantage their builders had of constructing them in the presence of the enemy.

In many respects, the whole Okinawan struggle resembled a World War I offensive in terms of the conditions the respective sides faced. Even so, the IJA cave systems had a personality different from the Western Front trench systems. The World War I trench systems did not put men continuously underground, nor were the major artillery pieces, rear headquarters, and rear-area supply personnel underground. It was the American air presence that forced the radical movement of these combat support elements underground, because the American planes carried a weapon deadlier than guns or bombs: perfect knowledge of Japanese activities. Any observed activity would be blasted off the face of the earth by remote fire.

There was another notable difference. Because of the undulating terrain, IJA units were able to build their forts into the hillsides while still giving a view on the world that was above ground level, and that seemed to and did dominate terrain. This, plus the fact that the caves were almost completely safe from bombardment, seems to have spared IJA soldiers some of the dismay that World War I soldiers experienced living day in and day out in the trenches. The Japanese soldiers did not suffer as much as the World War I soldiers from the "underground neuroses" described by Eric Leed. That the Americans never themselves went underground to engage in World War I-style mining and countermining (in effect underground maneuver combat) also may have saved the IJA soldier some mental stress.[20]

Okinawa Terrain

The IJA 32d Army chose to build its main defensive positions across the Okinawa isthmus near a line running from Uchitomari on the west coast to Tsuwa on the east (see map 3 in chapter 1). The rugged terrain in this area, which extended southward to the Naha-Yonabaru line, was superbly fitted to the methods the IJA had adopted of using hilltop pillbox caves and reverse-slope fields of fire that would force the Americans to engage as small infantry teams. The terrain here was rolling and hilly and "broken by terraces, steep natural escarpments, and ravines." It was

When U.S. forces fought their way over a ridge, they often found themselves in a tangle of irregular ground such as that shown here, honeycombed with reverse slope fire ports

characterized by "lack of pattern, steep slopes, and narrow valleys" and was "filled with twisting ridges and spotted with irregular knolls." Because the terrain was hilly and irregular, it provided innumerable short fields of fire but no long fields of fire. This was ideal for the Japanese whose defense relied on "large numbers of short-range weapons." The tangled, broken ground forced the Americans to fight a thousand small battles hand to hand instead of one large battle at a distance where their preponderant firepower would have given them the advantage.[21]

Cave War Tactics

The IJA 32d Army on Okinawa succeeded in doing what Robert E. Lee vowed, but failed, to do at Gettysburg: maneuver offensively but fight defensively. The 32d Army placed itself where it knew the U.S. Army must come, Okinawa, and it shrewdly chose terrain (1) that was strategically crucial for the Americans to capture for control of Nakagusuku Bay and Naha harbor, yet which also (2) was extremely favorable for the defender. (MacArthur had done the same on Bataan.) Having identified such terrain, the 32d Army thoroughly prepared it. Creating the cave environment was itself the 32d Army's greatest operational success.

The Japanese built the caves with fields of fire on reverse slopes and on important roadways and integrated the cave fire nets, though not as well as they might have.[22] Until U.S. ground forces reached the hidden defense line across the southern isthmus, the 32d Army stayed in its caves and did not respond to any air or sea reconnaissance efforts. The U.S. Tenth Army therefore did not know where on Okinawa the IJA 32d Army was. Scout planes could identify no IJA targets for the bombardment prior to landing. Even after landing, the U.S. Tenth Army moved about the island for eight days before it ran up against IJA 32d Army's main line of resistance at Kakazu and Minami-Uebaru.

Both the Japanese and the Americans had to accommodate themselves tactically to the existence of the caves. At first, the Americans did not know the pillbox caves even existed and had no doctrine for dealing with them. This was a severe disadvantage, but one for which the Americans on the line soon found a solution. The Americans at the outset of the offensive advanced en masse and were mowed down in crowds by cave-hidden machine guns when they reached the reverse slopes.[23] American officers on the scene quickly developed a method for avoiding these unhappy effects, however. They would bombard the Japanese positions they faced, forcing the IJA off the surface. They would then infiltrate men in small numbers through narrow gaps in the Japanese fixed cave fire line ("dead spaces"). The fact that the cave positions were separated and their fire nets not perfectly integrated became a serious Japanese liability here because the Americans took advantage of the small openings in the fire line to envelop the cave positions.[24]

Learning these countermethods took time and probably explains the heavy losses suffered by each American line division in its first two weeks of combat. Casualties for each American division's first two weeks of anti-cave fighting exceeded losses of subsequent weeks by 40 percent or more (see table 1). The only partial exception to this pattern was the 7th Infantry Division, which fought along the less densely defended eastern shoreline and which had already acquired prudent instincts for this type of ground action on Leyte.[25]

The Japanese countertactic to American ground infiltration was to leave more men on the surface during bombardment and to put still more men back on the surface instantly when the bombardment stopped. These troops would attack the few Americans who had seeped through the holes in the line and try, often successfully, to drive them back. The result was fierce small-arms fights between small units of men in isolated valleys not readily visible to either main force. These fights could be fairly equal because the Americans had only the light arms they could carry and could not use artillery because at close quarters they risked destroying their own precarious positions. Whenever the Americans could, however, they had tanks with them, which the Japanese did not. Losses in these all-important small-arms fights were high. The Americans often had to infiltrate men forward several times before they could gain a foothold that was proof against the aggressive Japanese counterattacks.[26]

The Japanese countermethods in some respects resembled the defensive tactics that evolved on the Western Front in World War I. Rather than attacking, the Japanese limited their efforts to counterattacking and struck only against those advanced enemy elements precariously established on the wrong side of the defense line. While the American attackers were still few and not dug in, a small IJA unit had to rush them boldly with small arms and quickly drive them out of their isolated strongpoint before they consolidated. They had to do what storm troops were invented to do in World War I. Japanese artillery also focused on the Americans' exposed positions before they could dig in.[27]

The fierce Japanese counterattacks were notoriously effective, and indeed it was here that the IJA's orthodox doctrine emphasizing bold and hasty attack served 32d Army well. The quick death-defying attacks by a platoon or a company, armed only with bolt-action rifles and knee mortars, was something IJA training had prepared 32d Army for well, even though that same training was inappropriate for all the rest of the Okinawa experience.

Tanks Versus Caves

Use of unaccompanied infantry against the cave positions was not very successful, and if this had been the Americans' only resource, their progress could have been stymied.[28] Indeed there could have been a stalemate on Okinawa despite the Americans' firepower, in which both sides dug in and neither side could move. What made it possible for the Americans to advance expeditiously against the IJA's ingenious caves was the tank. The tank did not make it easy to move through the densely entrenched fire-

TABLE 1

Average Weekly Battle Casualties of American Combat Divisions on Okinawa for First Two Weeks of Full Engagement and for All Subsequent Weeks of Full Engagement

Unit	First Two Weeks' Average Weekly Battle Casualties (A)	Subsequent Weeks' Average Weekly Battle Casualties (B)	Ratio of A to B
7th Infantry Division	695[a]	558[b]	1:24
27th Infantry Division	1,298[c]	—[d]	—
77th Infantry Division	905[e]	631[f]	1:43
96th Infantry Division	1,074[g]	575[h]	1:87
1st Marine Division	1,595[i]	679[j]	2:35
6th Marine Division	1,220[k]	880[l]	1:39

[a] Figures for 9—21 April.
[b] Figures for 22 April—23 June, but excluding figures for 6—26 May because the weekly numbers were affected by 7th Infantry Division's withdrawal from the line for rest on 10—22 May.
[c] Figures for 15—28 April.
[d] After suffering exceptionally high casualties in the late April offensives, the 27th Infantry Division was permanently withdrawn from the line on 1 May for mop-up and garrison duty in the north.
[e] Figures for 29 April—12 May.
[f] Figures for 13 May—2 June.
[g] Figures for 9—21 April.
[h] Figures for 22 April—23 June, but excluding figures for 29 April—12 May because the weekly numbers were affected by the 96th Infantry Division's withdrawal from the line for rest on 30 April—10 May.
[i] Figures for 29 April—12 May.
[j] Figures for 13 May—23 June.
[k] Figures for 6—19 May.
[l] Figures for 20 May—23 June.

Source: U.S. Army, 10th Army, G-1 Section, "G-1 Periodic Reports," Numbers 1 to 14 (Okinawa, 1 April 1945—7 July 1945).

swept zone, but it made it possible. The tanks provided the Americans with a kind of instant symmetrical answer to the caves in this kind of warfare. Tanks protected by infantry were able to duel with the gunport caves, which were also protected by infantry.

In other words the basic tactical unit on each side was a pillbox and accompanying infantry. The Americans used a mobile, slightly vulnerable pillbox, the tank, against the Japanese who used invulnerable but not mobile pillboxes, the caves. The Japanese overcame the immobility of the cave pillboxes somewhat by having caves everywhere and moving among them. As in World War I, much of the combat, despite the massive artillery activity, came to involve infantry battling fluidly around machine-gun strongpoints, only on the American side the strongpoints themselves were moving. In the end, these actions featured small-arms and mortar fights at company and platoon levels, sometimes hand to hand.[29]

Japanese Antitank Tactics

Even though Japanese antitank tactics were systematic, they were ultimately ineffective. Their failure, however, was not due to the Japanese' lack of information about American tanks. The 32d Army had anticipated the pivotal role of tanks on Okinawa: "fighting against the American land army is practically the same thing as fighting against...M4 tanks," 32d Army Directive No. 13 intoned.[30]

The Japanese forces were advised to wait until the American tanks were very close to their positions and then to open fire both on the tank with artillery and on the accompanying infantry with small arms and mortars. The Japanese antitank weapons included the 37-mm gun, which had a limited effect on the Sherman tank, and also the 47-mm antitank gun, which was effective. The 47-mm gun, designed in 1941 as a modern antitank weapon, had been distributed in limited numbers to Japanese 32d Army forces. It had a muzzle velocity of 2,700 feet per second, had rubber tires, and weighed 1,600 pounds, which meant it could be manhandled. In

IJA Model 1 (1941) 47-mm antitank gun

fact, the 47-mm guns were usually placed in cave pillboxes where they were not mobile, however.[31]

Even though the 47-mm gun would "perforate...any armor of the M4A6 tank...at all ranges...up to 800 yards," the Japanese doctrine in all cases was to withhold fire until the foe's tank team was quite close.[32] This saved the Japanese position longer from discovery and gave the 47-mm gun, if present, a surer shot. If no gun was available, the enemy tank, if allowed to approach unopposed, would be nearer to antitank infantry.[33]

Once the adversary tanks approached, IJA soldiers would unleash small-arms, mortar, and antitank artillery fire all at once to destroy both the tank and the infantry team. If no 47-mm guns were on hand or if the gun failed to destroy the tank, the IJA soldiers' next tactic was to drive the U.S. infantry away from the tank using small arms and mortars. This left the tanks "blind," as a Japanese tactical bulletin put it. The Japanese also attempted to kill the commander of an American tank if he was standing in the hatch.[34]

Captain Ito Koichi of the IJA 24th Division maintained that American Sherman tanks withdrew if they were fired on by light mortars, even though the mortars would not harm a Sherman. The reason, he believed, was that the American tankers could not distinguish the mortar shell explosions from more dangerous howitzer shell explosions. In reality, Captain Ito may have been witnessing the American tanks' efforts to stay with their infantry when the latter fell back to avoid mortar bombardment.[35]

Tanks that did not stay with their infantry were exposed to the IJA's third tactical step, which was to destroy the tank with hand-carried explosives—satchel charges, reinforced grenades, and mines. Most of these devices were powerful enough to damage a tread or the bogie wheels of a tank, thereby immobilizing it, but they were not powerful enough to breach the hull. The attackers tried to remain concealed until the first volley of small-arms fire had driven off American infantry, then they assaulted the tank. Often, the tanks' likely avenues of approach were mined so that the advancing tank might be immobilized by a preplaced mine.[36]

Immobilized tanks continued to be a main focus of struggle for the Japanese. Captain Ito claims that the most effective method of attack for lightly armed men against tanks was to immobilize the tank with a satchel charge or mine, then destroy it at leisure with Molotov cocktails. In fact American crews hastily abandoned stalled tanks, hoping to retrieve them after nightfall. Therefore Japanese engineers were advised to move in and blow up stalled tanks before nightfall. Sometimes the Japanese were content just to place mines around the damaged vehicle, especially in the likely direction of towing. (Japanese soldiers often laid mines in tread tracks at night, expecting the American tanks to use the same avenue again.) This gave IJA infantry a chance to ambush the expected tank towers.[37]

Japanese antitank tactics, in sum, involved (1) destroying the tank with an antitank gun, (2) driving off its infantry with small arms and destroying

IJA engineers sought to disable U.S. tanks using the minimal resources available

the tank with hand-carried explosives, or (3) immobilizing the tank and destroying it later. Conspicuously absent from their antitank system were bazookas. The Japanese had received some *Panzerfaust* (antitank) technology from the Germans but had not converted it into weapons. Also nearly absent was the antitank use of heavy artillery. The IJA had the artillery but did not have radio contact between the small line units in the front and the artillery in the rear that would have made attack on particular tanks possible. The lack of bazookas and radios (and the partial lack of 47-mm antitank guns) was extremely serious. The liberal presence of these items could have slowed the advance of the American tanks significantly and prolonged the Okinawa stalemate.

This Japanese failure to provide bazookas and radios was all the more serious because the modest technology and resources needed for both were available. If some of the resources devoted to well-machined field guns, howitzers, and mortars on Okinawa had been devoted instead to some humbler antitank gear, the battlefield might have been transformed. The inadequacy of IJA field equipment must be attributed in the end to doctrinal prejudice. Somehow, the IJA's conceptual approach to combat did not include or anticipate an armored adversary or an environment where a company's only possible link to the larger battlefield was by radio. These shortcomings are the more blameworthy since the IJA had had similar problems with the Russians at Nomonhan in 1939 but had done nothing about them.[38]

American Anticave Tactics

The Americans' tactics for destroying caves resembled Japanese tactics for destroying tanks. The Americans used artillery, flamethrowers, and small arms to drive in the caves' protective infantry, thus allowing friendly infantry to approach the cave and disable it so the whole cave position could then be destroyed at leisure. The result in practice was that, between bombardments, there were lethal firefights between small units of infantry to see which infantry could reach the other's hardened pillboxes, tanks, and caves.

The cave positions on Okinawa were a defensive masterpiece, impervious to all fire (except a direct hit on the gunport). This gave the IJA soldiers a false sense of security, however, and in the early days of battle, false tactics. Defenders found that despite the caves' strength against fire, they could easily be breached if surrounded by infantry. The caves had a limited field of vision, like tanks, so their occupants did not even know where attackers were.

To protect infantry from the crushing American bombardments, IJA companies were advised to draw all their men into the caves, except for two or three entries. But the unhappy result of this was that, when the bombardments ceased, American tank-infantry teams rushed forward to seize cave entrances, thus trapping whole companies and their weapons helplessly inside. Holding all IJA infantry safe in the caves was not as prudent as it first appeared.[39]

The Japanese response was to leave ten or twelve men per company outside, even during heavy bombardment. Their job was to survive the bombardment, then hold off the advancing American infantry long enough for their comrades to emerge from the cave to help hold the ground. The mature cave positions thus had interlocking fire and were screened by a system of foxholes that were manned at all times (see figure 7). There was not enough room between the caves to deploy the entire force under cover outside, however, so only one-third of the troops would be put outside when the bombardment stopped. This meant that the two-thirds of the troops remaining in the cave always risked being trapped helplessly underground.[40]

The Americans' method for reducing the caves, what they called Blowtorch and Corkscrew and the Japanese called "cavalry charge," was to bombard the cave, killing surface infantry or forcing them inside. This alone did not subdue the cave-protected infantry, so the Americans then approached with tanks and infantry teams. These together drove the remaining IJA infantry away from the cave entrances. Fire from the tanks' machine guns, main guns, or flamethrowers was used to push IJA gunners away from the cave fire ports long enough for U.S. infantry to get past

U.S. troops here try to reduce a cave fire port concealed in the notch of ground right of center. But they are within the firing zone of IJA infantrymen outside the cave and cannot move freely. Note the mortar shell burst on the rise of ground in the center.

their angles of fire into what the Japanese called the "dead angle." Actually, to increase firepower, the IJA often had riflemen fire at angles off the machine gun or cannon in the fire port. They called this "sleeve" tactics (see figure 9). In order to get into the dead spaces, the Americans had to first break through the Japanese infantry defense line. Once they had done that, though, the cave positions were completely helpless. The Japanese called this a "straddle" attack since American riflemen straddled the exits with their fire instead of standing directly in front of the exit openings where IJA soldiers could fire on them. The Americans could not fire in from these positions either, but they could shoot any Japanese trying to exit.[41]

Many of the caves were situated under the dome of a hill, with exits on the sides and the rear of the dome, and a fire port facing the front. The Japanese especially dreaded the Americans' advance to the top of the dome. The summit was outside the fire port's fire angle and often covered every exit, so that one American standing there with a machine gun could prevent all egress from the cave, despite its multiple exits. Even if no dome existed, the American infantry would sweep to the far side of the hill where the cave was and cover the rear slope exits so that inmates had no choice but to surrender. Usually the Americans tried to find the air shaft above a cave and throw in a phosphorus grenade, a smoke bomb, or other explosives. Sometimes, they would pump in large amounts of gasoline, which

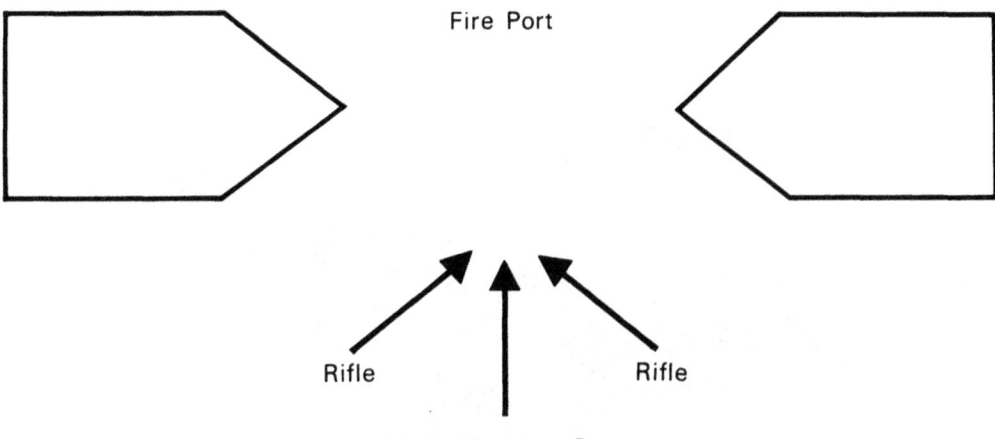

Figure 9. Sleeve-type position

they then ignited. These methods either killed the soldiers inside or forced them out. Having done this, the Americans either sealed the cave by blowing up the exits or occasionally entered it to take possession. With this, the caves were considered secure, and the Americans moved forward.[42]

Where caves were only haphazardly subdued, the IJA soldiers stationed inside continued to resist. The Americans' task was to seal every exit before nightfall. Often, however, they failed to find all the exits, or else they blew up an exit in a way that just widened the opening. In either case, the Japanese would escape from the exits after dark and engage in rear-area

U.S. troops preferred flame to drive off stubborn IJA defenders

Once U.S. troops got inside the angle of fire, a cave position was vulnerable. These troops have sprung a demolitions charge in a cave fire port, smoking at left.

attacks or return to their own lines. On the other hand, there were a few Japanese soldiers who dwelled quietly in their by-passed caves for months and surrendered only when Japan did, some time after the campaign in Okinawa concluded.[43]

In the tank-versus-cave warfare, a moving strongpoint—the tank—was pitted against a fixed strongpoint—the cave—with infantry moving fluidly to protect each.

Japanese Artillery

Although the Americans had firepower that greatly exceeded Japanese firepower in all categories, the Japanese 32d Army nevertheless had considerable artillery on Okinawa. The Japanese forces had confidence in their artillery, though the American experts who examined it after the battle were critical of certain features. To unify control over the artillery, it was all gathered into 32d Army's 5th Artillery Command under Lieutenant General Wada Kosuke, which included three artillery regiments, an artillery battalion, a mortar regiment, and two light mortar battalions. Besides these there were the 24th Division's artillery regiment and the 44th IMB's artillery battalion, both also placed under Wada's direction.[44]

All of these units together held 287 guns and 30 mortars of 70-mm bore or more for a total of 317 tubes, according to the count of U.S. Tenth Army intelligence after the battle. Inagaki Takeshi, a Japanese journalist who has investigated the Okinawa campaign, gives a figure of 470 tubes for 32d Army, a tally that apparently includes guns of smaller caliber. Inagaki notes that, when the front confined itself to a five-mile width of the Shuri isthmus, this was the heaviest concentration of Japanese guns in any Pacific campaign. Although there were a few 200-mm naval guns, most of the guns were either 75-mm or 150-mm.[45]

Japanese artillerists of the 1st Artillery Mortar Regiment used twenty-four 320-mm spigot mortars. These mortars, which had a range of three-quarters of a mile, fired shells that weighed 650 pounds and left a crater 15 feet wide and 8 feet deep. The Japanese staff officers believed, and with some justification, that these shells frightened the Americans. Even so, these amazing weapons produced few casualties, because they had a "terrific blast effect but practically no fragmentation." Men not quite close to the fifteen-foot crater were unharmed.[46]

The 32d Army's artillery, like its other branches, was constantly governed by the reality of American bombardment. Almost all the field guns were put in cave mouths, as well as its machine guns and antitank guns. The difference was that the artillery caves were larger and located in the interior of the Okinawa landmass, away from the battle line. The guns were rolled to the narrow fire port when in use and away from it when not. Some guns had steel rails or wooden planks on the cave floor to facilitate this. The gun crews lived in the rear of the caves of the guns they served, as the infantry did.[47]

Typical artillery position

Dummy artillery position

A few rear-area guns were left in the open, and some Japanese crews preferred this because they believed casualties were less in the case of American counterfire. Crews caught in a bombarded cave mouth could not disperse and suffered heavy losses, even though the guns themselves were often dug out and reused after a direct hit.[48] All antiaircraft guns had to be left in the open to preserve their field of fire, but they were then carefully camouflaged. For more protection, crews fashioned dummy guns and carriages of logs, and these guns were also carefully camouflaged. For American fliers, it was very difficult to tell the difference between the camouflaged real antiaircraft guns and the camouflaged wooden ones.[49]

The effect of all this artillery was nonetheless limited. The 5th Artillery Command was largely hamstrung by the weakness of its communications system. Japanese artillery relied on field telephone wire to transmit fire requests. This was the case between regimental observation posts of the 1st Medium Artillery Regiment and its gun emplacements, for example, in whose position, although the distances were not great, wires were left exposed and were not well distributed among different routes.[50]

Wire was also used between infantry battalion headquarters, where fire requests originated, and the 5th Artillery Command in the rear. (Units smaller than battalion had no communication system except messengers.) These wires were frequently cut by American bombardment during the day, forcing infantry needing artillery to rely on coded radio or on foot messengers. Radio transmission in code was slow, and reception was often

Large guns were moved on rails or planks

IJA 127-mm antiaircraft gun

Dummy antiaircraft gun covered with camouflage material

impossible when senders or receivers were deep in the caves. Runners were extremely slow. The consequence was that an artillery request normally took six hours to fulfill. Therefore there was virtually no close infantry support by the field artillery. There were general bombardments preparatory to the Japanese offensives of 12 April and 4 May, however.[51]

Japanese gunners customarily fired only a few rounds and then pulled the guns away from the cave mouths. They did this to avoid drawing devastating American counterfire. American forces used new GR-6 sound-locator devices to find the Japanese guns. Americans called the short firing time "sniping," which frustrated their efforts to get a bearing. When the Americans got a bearing, they would blanket the area with fire or else send in a cub reconnaissance plane to pinpoint the offending gun and try for a direct hit. The Japanese tried to ward off the cubs with antiaircraft fire or obstruct their observation with smoke, but not always successfully.[52]

The Japanese ordinarily fired at dusk, night, or dawn, also to minimize counterfire. Sometimes they fired spotter rounds at dusk so they would be on target during the night.[53] Most of the Japanese fire, however, was "prearranged fire . . . delivered by . . . map data uncorrected." Most of the Japanese' targets were unobserved and unobservable. Artillery battalions sometimes sent liaison officers to the infantry regiments they were supporting, but these officers were not forward observers, and indeed, the Japanese 5th Artillery Command did not have any forward observers with the infantry. Sometimes a few artillery personnel and an officer would infiltrate American lines at night to bring back map coordinates for suitable targets, but these fires also were then delivered by uncorrected map coordinates.[54]

The Japanese never massed their battery fires except for a major offensive, and they were criticized by the Americans for this. There were good reasons why the Japanese did not mass fires, however. Not only did massed fires draw counterfire, they wasted the limited ammunition supply. The 5th Artillery Command had only 1,000 rounds per tube; therefore, saturation fire was out of the question. Lieutenant General Wada had imposed a reasonable working maximum of fifty shells per day per gun. Besides that, radio and visual communication between guns was limited by their physical isolation underground so that fire coordination would have been difficult in any case.[55]

All in all, Japanese use of artillery was efficiently parsimonious. It was nevertheless flawed by lack of responsiveness to particular needs on the front line, a shortcoming that could have been largely overcome, despite cave emplacement, with a more effective communications system. The frontline infantry needed radios below the battalion level, and the artillerists in their caves needed antennas to receive their messages. To rely on runners moving several miles in the open to relay fire requests or fire observation meant that hitting targets of opportunity was out of the question. The 5th Artillery Command gunners were given credit for thorough use of preregistered fires. In the event that was all they were able to achieve. The Japanese amassed a large artillery force on Okinawa, but because of limited ammunition and communications, and forced segregation underground, sniping was the most it could do.

Attack and Retreat, May 1945

Tactical methods on the Shuri line followed the tanks-versus-caves pattern through most of the Okinawa campaign. Tactical realities suddenly changed, however, on the morning of 4 May, when much of the IJA 32d Army left its caves to launch a major assault on U.S. lines. The Japanese decision to leave their safe cave fortresses for attack was, and still is, controversial. Both the issues and the personalities surrounding the 4 May offensive were similar to those of the modest 12 April offensive. However, pressure from IGHQ and 10th Area Army, a crucial element in the 12 April decision, was absent this time. Instead, Chief of Staff Cho and Operations Officer Yahara collided directly over what for 32d Army was a perpetual dilemma of doctrine.

On 22 April, the IJA 24th Division and the 44th IMB had been moved north to support the deteriorating 62d Division, displacing its right flank and forming a second line in its left rear respectively. Colonel Yahara, having at last resolved the north-south problem and formed a sturdy defensive line, was content with the situation. The 32d Army was implementing the kind of solid attrition defense Yahara had envisioned from the start. Despite their 10-to-1 advantage in firepower and 2-to-1 advantage in manpower, the Americans' advance was being held to a modest 100 yards per day. Moreover, by the end of April, the 32d Army had become the only Japanese force to maintain organized resistance to an American island landing for over thirty days.

Yahara's optimism about 32d Army's achievements was shared by only a minority of the 32d Army Staff, however. Most of the other members suffered from a growing feeling of gloom, which fueled a growing sentiment for a bold attack that might break them out of the status quo. Unlike Yahara, who thought they were doing well with what they had, other members were preoccupied with absolute failure. The 32d Army was being pushed inexorably back, and the eventual result of the current policy would be that all of them would perish and Okinawa would be lost. The somber mood of the staff was aggravated by conditions in the headquarters cave. American lines were getting closer, and shells fell thick around its entrances. Repeatedly, sentries posted there were killed. Smoke from exploding shells was pulled into the ventilator shaft, which caused great consternation when someone would yell "gas attack," sending the whole complement running for gas masks. The inherent stress of the situation, especially the element of certain death, was beginning to take its toll on everyone.[1]

The 29 April Meeting

In this environment, Lieutenant General Cho called a staff meeting on 29 April to discuss operations. Cho spoke firmly in favor of an offensive, for he had apparently made up his mind well before the meeting since he had already on 27 April asked Major Jin, the staff member in charge of air strategy, to begin research on a possible advance. Cho argued that in the present state of affairs, the Americans had the upper hand. If the status quo continued, the 32d Army eventually would be wiped out. The solution was to use their surplus resources for an offensive while they still could. In this way, they might break out of the current deadlock and avoid certain defeat.[2]

At this meeting, only Yahara spoke for continuing the war of attrition and avoiding an offensive. Yahara pointed out that in modern warfare a superiority of 3 to 1 was usually needed for successful attack. "To take the offensive with inferior forces . . . is reckless and would lead to certain defeat," he said. Second, the high ground around Minami-Uebaru had already fallen into American hands, giving them a major advantage in defensive terrain. Third, Yahara argued, a hasty offensive would fail, with thousands needlessly lost. Then, 32d Army's reduced forces would be unable to hold Okinawa for a long period and unable to delay the U.S. invasion of Japan. A hasty attack would cause 32d Army to fail in its duty.[3]

Major Jin, the aviation staff member, then spoke. Jin had favored greater efforts to protect the Yontan and Kadena airfields from the start. Jin, like Cho, described the need for an offensive and its possible success. The other young staff members were silent. Cho then declared again that he hoped for an attack to snatch life from the midst of death. At this, Yahara left the room. All the other staff members then agreed to launch an offensive.[4]

The 29 April staff meeting was as bitterly argued as the two earlier strategy meetings on 3 and 10 April had been. Like the April meetings, it did not settle the issue for Yahara. He continued to oppose an offensive, and Cho continued to favor one. Cho then tried this time to manage Yahara by sheer emotional force. At dawn on 30 April, before Yahara "had time to splash water on his face," Cho appeared at his quarters. Cho squeezed Yahara's hand and said with genuine enthusiasm that there had been nothing but trouble between them in the past and that they would probably both die together on Okinawa. Cho then asked if Yahara, on this one occasion, would go along with the offensive. As Cho spoke, his tears fell abundantly. Yahara was deeply moved, despite his aloof reputation, and before long he was weeping too. He was overcome by Cho's sudden display of emotion and said, "I consent."[5]

Lest this dose of sentimental pressure still not be enough, Lieutenant General Ushijima, commander of 32d Army, took Yahara aside in the staff room the same day and sternly counseled him not to undermine support for the attack. Mild-mannered Ushijima never spoke to anyone in this way, and Yahara sensed that Cho was also behind this chastisement. Yahara said he thought the offensive was a meaningless suicide attack but that he would support it since it was decided. Ushijima replied quietly that, of course, the offensive would be an honorable death attack.[6]

Even Yahara went along with the attack plans by the end of April, in public at least. There are a number of reasons why an immediate offensive was decided on even though its military use was doubtful. One of these was Cho's forceful personality, which sometimes simply overwhelmed those about him. Another was that the received doctrine of the IJA for many years had been to secure quick victory by attack, especially flank attack followed by close fighting. Cadets at the IJA Academy were taught that one Japanese division with a robust spirit of attack could defeat three Soviet divisions with superior equipment. Officers raised in this tradition had an exaggerated faith in the effectiveness of attack. Such habits of mind no doubt contributed to 32d Army's decision for an offensive.[7]

A third reason for the 32d Army's decision to attack was the spirit of gloom surrounding the staff. The staff's feeling of frustration at their resources being worn down to naught by the American advance caused them all to welcome a long-odds gamble that would at least give them hope. The attack would provide psychological relief from the stress of continuous defeat. Unfortunately, this was relief for the 32d Army Staff only. The 62d Division, steadily in combat, suffered stresses worse than the psychological kind and, in any case, was not to be active in the offensive. The 24th Division, meant to carry out the attacks, had felt no stress needing relief because it had not yet been exposed to combat. On this point, the 32d Army Staff may be criticized. Its mounting of a major offensive to relieve its own psychological discomfort was improper.[8]

Honorable Death Attack and Ritual Suicide

After the 29 April meeting, Ushijima spoke for the first time in terms of an honorable death attack. Honorable death (*gyokusai*) and ritual disembowelment (*seppuku* or *hara-kiri*), self-destruction for units and individuals respectively, were a powerful part of Japanese military culture. Honorable death, literally "smashing the [imperial] jewel," meant that a unit fought until its last member died in combat, resisting the temptation to flee or surrender. Every school child was taught famous historical instances of the phenomenon. The concept probably evolved out of the conditions of Japan's Warring States period (1470–1600), when whole units sometimes fled or changed sides, but where the samurai closest to their feudal masters were expected to fight to the death and where soldiers were normally tortured and killed if taken alive. The Japanese may have felt more threatened than other societies by the possibility that the ordinary soldier would flee from battle and therefore had strong injunctions against flight. Being captured also raised a suspicion of disloyalty and selfishness. The samurai or officer who quit fighting to surrender put his personal convenience ahead of his cause, which showed a deeply flawed character. Related to this was the traditional treatment of war prisoners, which was that they were either killed, tortured and killed, or incarcerated with so few amenities that they soon died in captivity. That prisoners were worthy of respect and might be exchanged was an idea that did not exist in the Japanese mind. Rather, the Japanese believed, and with no soul searching, that for a unit to perish in combat was both very honorable and very expedient.

The notion of individual suicide for soldiers derived from similar considerations. The samurai or officer in danger of being captured alive was expected to take his own life, according to proper ritual forms if possible. If honorable death attacks failed, the officer and, in the 1940s, the private soldier as well, were obliged to commit suicide. This showed sincerity, avoided harsh captivity, and prevented the enemy from using captives to manipulate those still uncaptured. The tradition of suicide also may have relieved psychological stress, paradoxically, because its suffering was brief, self-administered, and held no loss of dignity, and because the soldier entering combat knew from the outset that nothing worse than that need happen to him. Suicide to avoid capture also helped guarantee normal military benefits for the victim's surviving family.

The IJA 32d Army thought increasingly in terms of honorable death attack and suicide in the latter part of the Okinawa campaign. Honorable death and ritual suicide held not only a practical military appeal but also a romantic appeal because of popular cultural traditions. Yahara opposed premature resort to honorable death, however, and often said so. He felt it was self-indulgent to make operational decisions because of romantic sentiment toward suicide and equally self-indulgent to seek an early and glorious escape instead of facing the heavy operational burdens still at hand.

Preparing the 4 May Offensive

Once the commanders had agreed on an offensive and formally scheduled it for 4 May, it was up to Yahara to draft the plans with the help of staff members Nagano and Kusumaru. Yahara performed this task diligently but still had not abandoned his wish to minimize the ill effects of the offensive, and so he inserted a minor change likely to have a major consequence. The ambitious battle plan, in eight items, provided for counterlandings in the American rear by the 23d and 26th Shipping Engineer Regiments on the east and west coasts respectively (see map 7). The 62d Division, holding the left half of the Japanese line, was to maintain its position, then go on the offensive once attacking units on its right had broken through. The 24th Division was to provide the main weight of the offensive and punch through on the right half of the line. The preparatory barrage was to begin at 0450, on 4 May, and last for thirty minutes. The 24th

Division was then expected to sweep past the Tanabaru escarpment to the Minami-Uebaru hill and eventually reach Futema.[9]

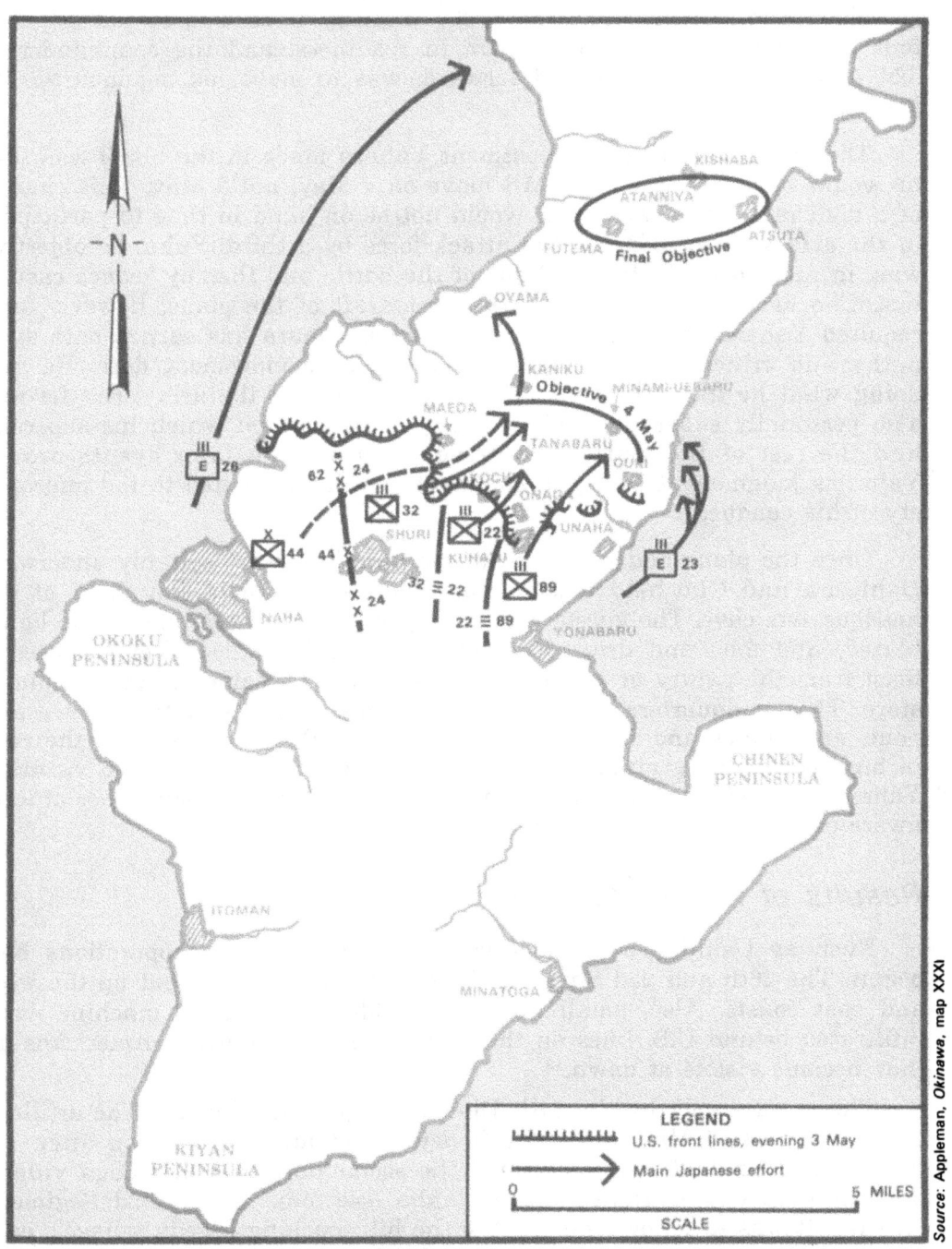

Map 7. Plan for the IJA 4 May offensive

The 44th IMB was to shift on 3 May from its reserve line behind the 62d Division to a position northeast of Shuri. On 4 May when the 24th Division went forward, the 44th IMB was to drive northwest through the opening to the coast town of Oyama, thus cutting off the U.S. 1st Marine Division from retreat. Also, the IJN's infantry force was to put together four elite battalions and hold them in readiness, and the commander of 32d Army, as the lines moved forward, was to move his headquarters to Maeda.[10]

The small, but critical, adjustment Yahara made in the plans was that he would have had the 44th IMB move on 4 May, not 3 May. This change of a digit meant that 44th IMB would not be on hand in time to participate in the attack, thus reducing the attack force by a third. Yahara's objective was, in fact, to hold 44th IMB out of the battle and thereby reduce casualties. Cho caught the change in the first draft of the plans, however, and required Yahara to restore the original date. Yahara has earned both sympathy and criticism for altering the 44th IMB's movement date. He was doing what he thought was in the best interests of the army. But he was also personally subverting duly promulgated orders on which his superiors and the rest of the staff had agreed. Even though later events proved Yahara's judgment to be right, commentators have pointed to the impropriety of his conduct.[11]

Once the plans had been set and preparations were suitably underway, Ushijima and Cho held a previctory banquet in their chambers of the headquarters cave. The guests were nine general officers only. Electric lights blazed, and food and drink were plentiful. Cho's skilled chef prepared a feast from the pantry of canned goods. Fine Scotch came out of Ushijima's store. The headquarters office girls came dressed attractively to serve and pour, and smiles and laughter were inexhaustible. Ushijima and the rest, in high spirits, congratulated each other on the next day's certain victories. Yahara was reminded of Wellington's ball before Waterloo, and other officers aware of the banquet perhaps were too.[12]

Results of the 4 May Offensive

Even as Ushijima's banquet was going on, offensive operations had begun. The 26th and 23d Shipping Engineer Regiments set out up the west and east coasts. Also, small groups of soldiers with light machine guns infiltrated behind U.S. lines on the night of 3 May to attack Americans as they became visible at dawn.[13]

The main attack by the 24th Division began on schedule. The artillery opened at 0450, 4 May, and 24th Division's advance began soon after. By 0530, 89th Regiment had penetrated the sector northeast of Onaga village and attacked on the right toward Unaha (see map 8). The 32d Regiment on the left was to follow and capture the hill touching Maeda village's east end and then move forward to take the Tanabaru escarpment. The 22d Regiment in the 24th Division's center was to go forward and lay smoke,

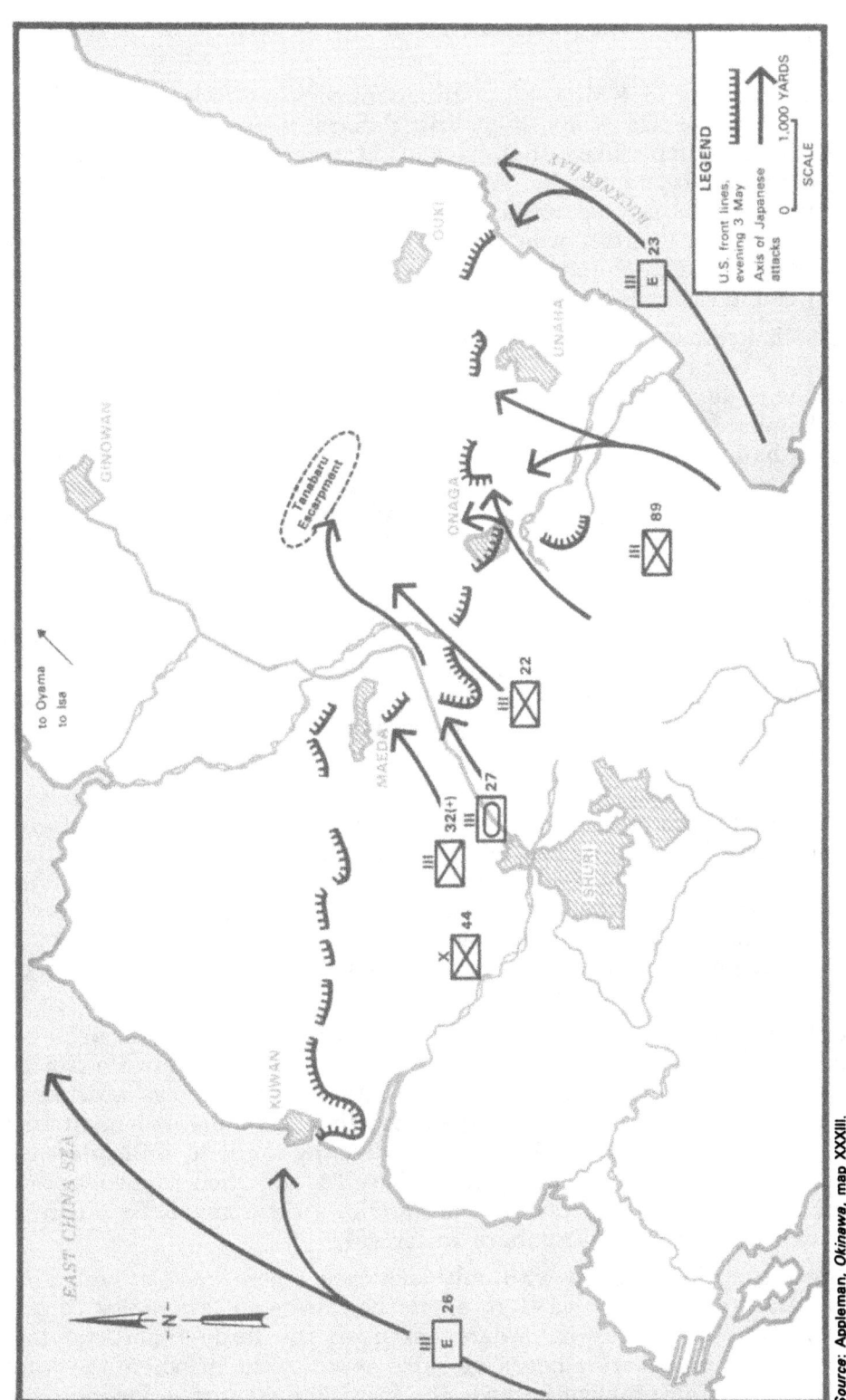

Source: Appleman, *Okinawa*, map XXXIII.

Map 8. The IJA 4 May offensive

then attack toward Onaga, joining itself to the left flank of the 89th Regiment.[14]

On the morning of 4 May, all of this seemed to go forward splendidly. The staff officers of 32d Army, including Yahara, were all smiles and congratulations. Ushijima joked that perhaps it was now time to move his headquarters forward to Maeda. After noon, realistic battle reports began to come in from the combat units, however, and spirits were again dampened. Adding to this effect was the fact that the Japanese artillery fire that had dominated in the morning no longer did so, and instead a heavy American counterbombardment had begun.[15]

The 89th Regiment on the far right had moved forward a few thousand yards before being blocked by the U.S. 7th Infantry Division. The 89th Regiment was damaged severely in the open by concentrated land, naval, and air bombardment: it lost half its strength. The IJA 22d Regiment in the center had even less luck, its advance being delayed by its task of laying smoke, and it suffered especially when the smoke unexpectedly cleared. American sources say the attacks were contained by 0800 on 4 May, and Japanese sources indicate that forward movement on the right had ceased by 1200.[16]

On the left flank of the 24th Division's line, the 32d Regiment was supposed to capture Maeda hill, then sweep forward and secure the Tanabaru escarpment. The 32d, however, became entangled with the rightmost elements of the IJA 62d Division (see map 6 in chapter 2), causing the confused combat in the vicinity of Maeda hill to become more so, and the attack on Maeda failed.[17]

Meanwhile, the 44th IMB was in position northwest of Shuri ready to begin its drive toward Oyama as soon as the 32d Regiment opened a breach in the American lines. Saddened by the great casualties and by the failure of the 24th Division's attacks, Major General Suzuki, commander of the 44th IMB, asked to be thrown into the assault. Yahara told him, however, that Maeda hill was not yet sufficiently occupied for the 44th to move. It would only heighten the needless sacrifice and still not achieve a strategic breakthrough.[18]

On the night of 4–5 May, the 32d Regiment, 24th Division, achieved an unexpected success, however. Its 1st Battalion, under Captain Ito Koichi, had arbitrarily abandoned the hopeless frontal attacks it was ordered to make during the day and instead spent its time carefully reconnoitering the American positions. This allowed it during the night to infiltrate eastward across the Ginowan-Shuri road undetected and then to penetrate a half mile into the American rear to the Tanabaru escarpment. By dawn on 5 May, Ito's battalion held Tanabaru in force.[19]

Achieving brilliant results with only lackluster orders was not accidental with Captain Ito. He observed that, since there were so few radios in use, the 32d Army Staff made its orders based on the tardy reports of foot messengers. The orders were based on false assumptions of where the front line was, a recurring problem because the front line was irregular, not continuous, and constantly shifting. Ito thus acquired the habit of walking his lines each night to discover where his and the Americans' positions were. This allowed him to adjust his response to orders in an advantageous manner. This method, although unorthodox, stood Ito's battalion in good stead on 4 May.[20]

The IJA 27th Tank Regiment was also active in the Maeda hill sector at the left end of the 24th Division's line. This was the only occasion where the Japanese used tanks in an offensive role on Okinawa. The tank regiment also had little success trying to break through at Maeda, however. It penetrated to the far side of the Maeda heights on 5 May but was unable to contact the infantry unit there that was supposed to support it in the joint attack. It therefore returned to its 4 May positions. Some Japanese observers felt the 27th Tank Regiment had achieved an advantageous position on Maeda hill during the day of 4 May and that it and the supporting infantry elements in the area therefore ought not have been recalled the next day. Nevertheless, when the 27th Tank Regiment did withdraw, it had only six tanks remaining, all of which were then converted to earth-covered pillboxes southwest of Shuri.[21]

The 26th and 23d Shipping Engineer Regiments fared even worse than the tank units. The 26th Engineers were supposed to move up the west coast on the night of 3—4 May and land at Oyama, well behind the American lines. There they were to link up with the 44th IMB when it swept into Oyama. The 26th Shipping Engineer Regiment mistook its mark, however, and turned into the coast at Kuwan, a point lying just behind the American front line and heavily defended. At 0200, elements of the U.S. 1st Marine Division opened fire on the barges of the 26th Engineers and fired machine guns abundantly on the Japanese trying to reach shore over the reefs. All of the boats were destroyed, and the few IJA soldiers who reached Kuwan were easily mopped up. A fragment of the 26th landed farther north at Isa, but these too were easily destroyed.[22]

The 23d Shipping Engineer Regiment, moving along the east coast at the same time, did no better. It landed just behind the U.S. 7th Infantry Division line near Ouki as planned but being exposed on the flat coastland was easily contained and destroyed by the 7th Division.[23]

The Japanese staff, however, had no knowledge of these disasters, apparently because the shipping units were in too much disarray to report. During the morning of 4 May the staff still assumed the counterlanding forces were enjoying success, and on 5 May these units were called back by radio, even though by that time they had ceased to exist. They "disregarded the order and fought to the last man," as an IJA staff officer later put it, though, in fact, they had "fought to the last man" the day before.[24]

By 5 May the forward motion of the 24th Division's offensive had completely stopped. The depleted 62d Division on the western half of the isthmus had not been able to move at all. The 44th IMB, though poised for action, was not even sent on its planned arc northwest to Oyama. The only bright spot was that, at dawn, the 1st Battalion of the 32d Regiment, 24th Division, under Captain Ito Koichi, held the Tanabaru escarpment.

When the 1st Battalion reached the Tanabaru heights, it sent a visual light signal to 32d Army, since its radio cryptographers had been lost. But Colonel Yahara doubted on the basis of this one signal that they were really there. Since Yahara administered operations, this guaranteed that Ito's battalion would remain unsupported and isolated. Yahara always erred on the side of caution, and Ito somehow always survived it.[25]

The Tanabaru escarpment. Captain Ito Koichi's 1st Battalion, 32d Regiment, held this position on 5—6 May.

At dawn on 5 May, the American forces counterattacked Ito and a fierce firefight ensued that lasted two days. The IJA 1st Battalion dug in on the heights, reoccupied the caves in the area, and vigorously defended them when the U.S. 17th Infantry Regiment counterattacked. The Japanese used machine guns, mortars, grenades, and a 75-mm pack howitzer they had brought with them, as well as captured American weapons. They cut telephone wires between the U.S. 17th Infantry Regiment and its battalions and cut off all access of that regiment to its own rear through the town of Tanabaru. On the night of the 6th, Ito's men made their way back to Japanese lines in accord with an order issued to them at noon on 6 May. The U.S. 17th Infantry Regiment calculated that the IJA 1st Battalion had lost 462 men.[26]

Overall, the news on 5 May was so discouraging that, at 1800, Ushijima, the 32d Army commander, took it on himself to suspend the entire offensive and recalled all units to their pre-4 May positions. He thus spared Cho and other staff officers from having to make this humiliating decision. Ushijima summoned Yahara and told him of the planned retreat. That night, the order was sent by coded radio to all units. Ushijima told Yahara that Yahara had been right after all, that the attack had failed, and that he would give Yahara more latitude in the future. He said that he had promised Minister of the Army Sugiyama and IJA Chief of Staff Umezu that he would not execute a premature honorable death attack and that, although the army had suffered heavy casualties, he would fight on with the remaining forces. Cho also rose to this occasion and helped soothe the anger and frustration of Jin and the others over halting the attack on which so much had been wagered. The young staff officers gave in temporarily to tears of despair.[27]

In fact, the casualties suffered in the 4 May offensive were quite large, even though there were no operational gains. In two days, the 32d Army had lost 7,000 men of its original 76,000-man force. The 62d Division had only one-fourth of its strength remaining, the 24th Division three-fifths, and the 44th IMB four-fifths. Moreover, the capability of the 5th Artillery Command was sharply reduced. Many of its tubes were lost because they were moved out of their caves toward the front lines to give better support for the offensive. Besides that, a large volume of shells had been expended so that the daily ration of shells per gun was reduced from fifty to fifteen per day. Overall, artillery firepower was thus reduced to about 50 percent of its original strength.[28]

All in all, while the 4—5 May offensive was a catastrophe, it was a brilliant catastrophe in the sense that it was a bold and imaginative stroke. It was useful for morale before it happened because it gave hope to staff members who were aware of the plans for it. It also may have had some value in keeping American commanders off-balance, forcing them to keep more guard details in rear areas and the like, though there is little evidence of this. A bold surprise is often advantageous in a campaign, even against long odds. That proved not to be the case for the 4 May offensive, however. The Japanese lost precious troops and materiel and, from then on, would have to rely more and more on converted service forces. The spirit of hope was also a casualty. A pall of gloom settled back on the 32d Army Staff after the 4 May offensive, and it never lifted.

The 29 May Withdrawal

After the suspension of the 4 May offensive, American forces again took the initiative and made deep incursions into the Japanese lines along both the east and west coasts. By 22 May, the 32d Army Staff was again debating what should be done. The answer that ultimately emerged was that all of 32d Army would withdraw to the Kiyan Peninsula in the south, form a new line, and fight on. The withdrawal would demonstrate two characteristic features of 32d Army's performance: first, its being torn still between romantic self-sacrifice and rational economy of force, and second, its aptitude for deft and effective maneuver in stressed circumstances.

After the failure of the 4 May offensive, 32d Army's only plan was to hold its lines. Since that approach was failing, Cho and others decided an appeal should be made to IGHQ for a massive air attack on the American fleet that would disrupt the U.S. Tenth Army's supply and cause its advance to falter. Major Jin Naomichi, the aviation staff officer, was ordered on 10 May to carry this plea to Tokyo. Jin was also to report on the state of affairs on Okinawa and the combat lessons learned. Yahara, although he did not interfere, opposed this plan on the grounds that with six divisions ashore, the American campaign would not be much affected by such additional air support as IGHQ could muster. The ten aggressive kamikaze attacks already launched on U.S. shipping around Okinawa had had only a limited effect on the ground fighting. Moreover, Yahara felt it would appear self-serving to ask that planes husbanded for the final defense of the homeland be used up instead on the Okinawa campaign. Yahara nonetheless attended Jin's farewell at Shuri and gave him a notebook to deliver to his father-in-law, a retired IJA lieutenant general. Jin was supposed to return to Tokyo by seaplane, but when the plane was unable to put down because of rough water, he set out by night in an ordinary fishing boat. The main consequence of Jin's voyage to Tokyo was that he himself, a leading advocate of sacrificial attack, survived the Okinawa campaign. News of his safe arrival in Tokyo caused some ambiguous feelings among his colleagues who remained in harm's way, however.[29]

Soon after Jin's departure, another sign appeared indicating that 32d Army's days were numbered. Several dozen young women were present in the Shuri cave headquarters, as they might be in any secure IJA office facility, working at routine clerical tasks. The staff members felt that, although it was their duty to die with the army, it was not the duty of these young women to do so. The women were therefore ordered to make their way out of the Shuri underground and rejoin the civilian elements of the Okinawa population. The young women protested that they were prepared to die when they came to the headquarters and that they were being sent away just because they were women. Nonetheless, they were made to feel they had to obey the commander's order and depart. As they scrambled out of the cave with their rucksacks in tow, the soldiers shouted after them things like "you may get yourself killed, but don't let anything happen to that fabulous face." This helped relieve the tension for a while. Ushijima and Cho, sensing the end, gave the young women as personal gifts their few treasured items of fine ceramic ware.[30]

Meanwhile, the U.S. Tenth Army resumed its offensive on 11 May. Through sustained pressure and hard fighting for particular objectives such as Conical Hill on the east coast and Sugar Loaf on the west coast, the Americans pushed the whole Japanese line back a half mile by 21 May. They achieved especially deep lodgments on the two extreme flanks, which was their intention. Especially on the eastern flank, elements of the U.S. 96th Infantry Division had probed as far as Sugar Hill and were close to turning the Japanese flank at Yonabaru.[31]

Reverse slope of Wana Ridge. U.S. forces captured this position only 1,000 yards northwest of the Shuri command cave on 21—23 May.

The 32d Army faced the same situation it had in mid-April. Its line was crumbling at both ends and about to collapse. This time, however, there were no reserves available to bring forward, once more placing the 32d Army Staff in a dilemma. Yahara, who had responsibility for the army's operations, felt withdrawal to the Kiyan Peninsula would be best. By this time, however, his relations with Cho had become so adversarial that he dared not even mention this solution. Instead he arranged for a junior staff member, Major Nagano Hideo, to submit to Cho a short position paper that spelled out abundant pros and cons but tended to favor the Kiyan withdrawal. Cho characteristically preferred an unyielding defense of the Shuri area where the 32d Army already was.[32]

To resolve the question, Cho convened a meeting of all major unit chiefs of staff on 22 May. The meeting considered three proposals. The first was to encircle Shuri and prepare a concentrated defense. Such a position would be too concentrated to hold the 50,000 surviving troops and the many long-range guns that were still intact, however. Moreover, such a restricted area would be extremely vulnerable to artillery fire.[33]

The second option considered was to withdraw from the Shuri line to the Chinen Peninsula. The Chinen was favorable as defensive terrain. It offered obstacles to easy tank movement and was encircled by sea and cliffs that would make amphibious envelopment more difficult. But the Chinen did not have good road access, which would hamper Japanese transport. Besides that, the Americans, who were already breaking through on the east, threatened the withdrawal routes to the eastward-lying Chinen Peninsula. The main difficulty with the Chinen, however, was that its defenses had been developed earlier by the relatively small 44th IMB. It therefore did not have caves enough or stored stockpiles enough to accommodate the entire 32d Army.[34]

The third possibility was to withdraw and form a line across the Kiyan Peninsula. The Kiyan had two defensible peaks, Yaeju-Dake and Yuza-Dake. Much of the coastal front was protected by thirty- to forty-meter-high precipices to frustrate amphibious landings in the rear. Having been developed by the larger 24th Division, the Kiyan had caves and stockpiles enough to provide for the entire 32d Army. The major disadvantage was that much of the terrain was open and even, thus allowing tanks to move freely. This terrain defect was the more serious since by this time 32d Army's antitank guns and mines, and for that matter its best antitank soldiers, already had been lost.[35]

Each chief of staff at the 22 May meeting was asked which alternative his unit favored. Colonel Ueno, chief of staff of the 62d Division, spoke first, in urgent tones. He said that the 62d Division had nearly exhausted its resources, above ground and below, and lacked the energy and means for a withdrawal. Moreover, the division had several thousand wounded that it could not bear to leave behind. Therefore, the men in the 62d Division wished to be allowed honorable death on the Shuri line. Most of their friends had already died there. The other 32d Army Staff officers, hearing Colonel Ueno's plea, were deeply moved.[36]

The chief of staff of the 24th Division, Colonel Kitani, then spoke, describing the advantages of moving the army to the Kiyan Peninsula. He pointed out that the 24th Division's 24th Transportation Regiment still had eighty trucks intact that could be used to move the army. A staff officer of the 44th IMB then gave his opinion in favor of moving the army to the Chinen Peninsula. In fact, each unit's chief of staff wished the new line placed in the area where each unit had developed its own respective fortifications before the battle began. Each unit apparently wished to fight on familiar ground and in familiar works.[37]

After the meeting was dismissed Yahara carried his recommendation to Cho, not changed by the meeting, that 32d Army should withdraw to a new line across the Kiyan Peninsula. He challenged the point of view of Colonel Ueno and the 62d Division that they should fight on around Shuri. He said that seeking honorable death at Shuri because comrades had died there was pure sentimentality. The Shuri position, once surrounded, would be indefensible and lead to a military disaster. Okinawa forces would fail to delay the coming struggle for the homeland. To die casually and with no good results was barbaric. The army's policy had to be realistic, and that meant moving to the Kiyan Peninsula.[38]

Yahara was evidently braced for another struggle with Cho over whether spiritual or operational priorities should prevail, but unnecessarily. The likable and unpredictable Cho straightforwardly agreed with the recommendation and wisely refrained from commenting on the argument. Retreat to Kiyan thus became 32d Army's policy on the next day, 23 May, when endorsed by Commander Ushijima. Movement of the wounded and munitions was to begin at once.[39]

The 32d Army Staff was eager to conduct the retreat from Shuri in such a way that the Americans did not break through the Shuri line and destroy the Japanese forces in detail while they were moving. In fact the Japanese would be so successful at this that the Americans had no idea a retreat was taking place until the day before it was completed. The 32d Army Staff was especially concerned that the Americans' deep inroads along the east coast near Yonabaru might produce an American breakthrough at the east end of the line. The U.S. 77th Infantry Division in that case could sweep westward and cut off the Japanese retreat, thus encircling large portions of the Japanese force, which would be caught in the open.

To prevent this, the remaining men of the 62d Division were to withdraw behind the Shuri lines on 25 May and attack the Yonabaru salient, thus containing the U.S. 77th Infantry Division and pushing it back away from the retreat routes (see map 9). This would allow the retreat of the

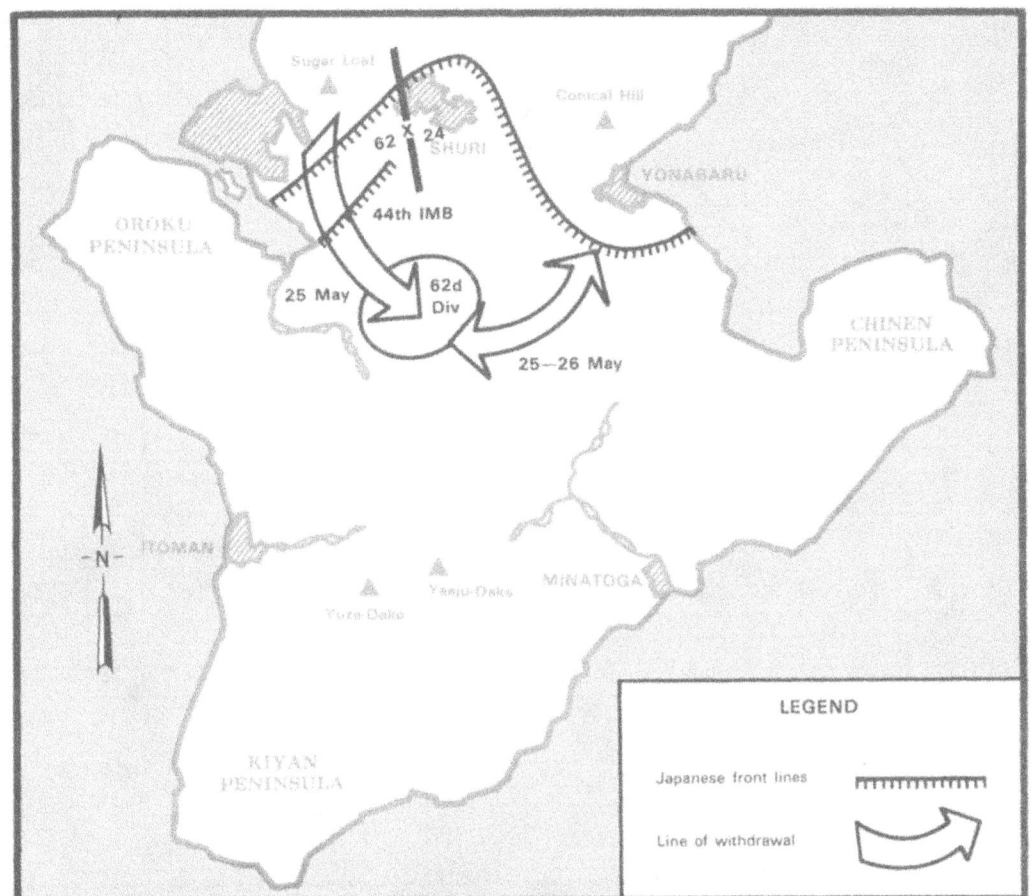

Map 9. Preliminary withdrawal of the 62d Division, 25 May 1945

main IJA line units on 29 May. In the event IJA 62d Division withdrew south of Shuri on the night of 24—25 May and did attack American positions at Yonabaru on the night of 25—26 May. This did not hurl the Americans back, but it did slow the U.S. 77th Infantry Division's forward progress and prevented its achieving an untimely breakthrough. The impression this made on the American commanders, who were unaware of the imminent retreat, was that the Japanese were fighting fiercely to maintain existing lines.[40]

After the east flank was somewhat stabilized, the IJA 24th Division pulled back from the northeast part of the line to the southwest on 29 May (see map 10). The 44th IMB pulled away from the northwest part of the line to the southeast on 31 May (see map 11). The 62d Division completed its withdrawal from its intermediate lines south of Shuri to a reserve area south of the new Kiyan lines on 4 June (see map 12). The 24th Division was also required to leave behind a screening force, which fell back to successively southward positions according to a timetable, reaching the Kiyan position also on 4 June.[41]

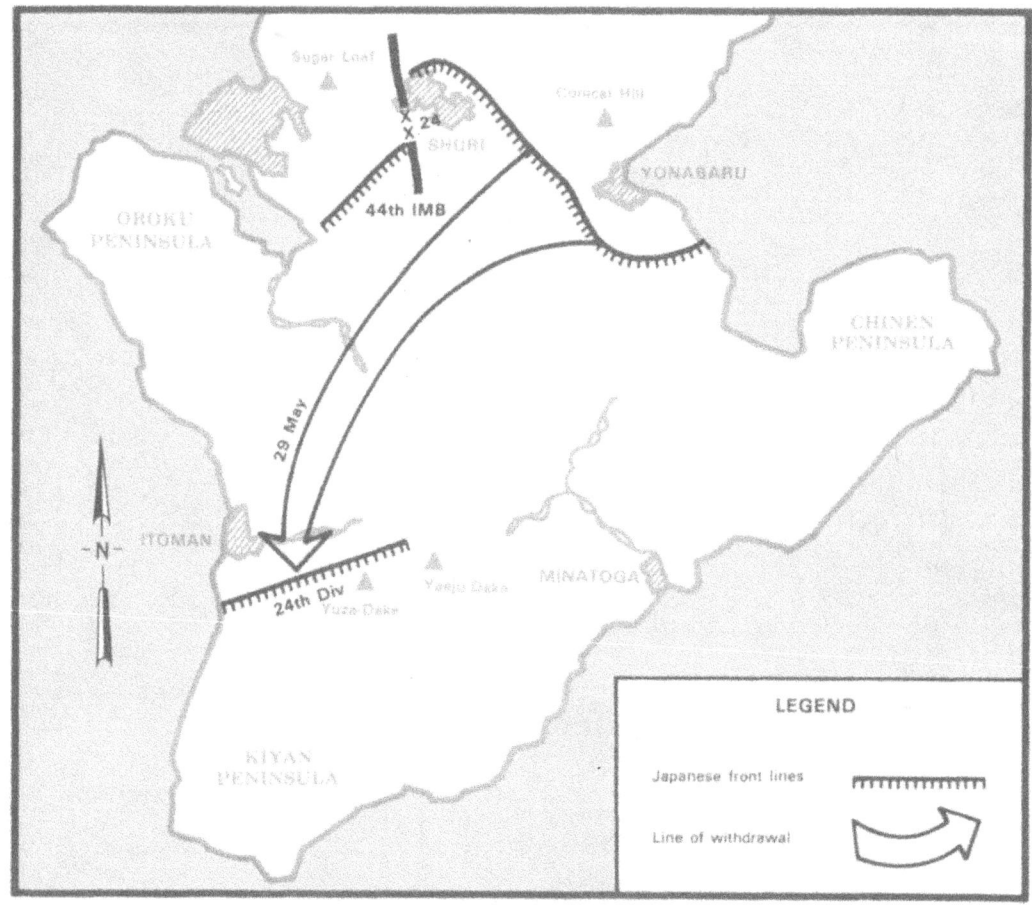

Map 10. Withdrawal of the 24th Division, 29 May 1945

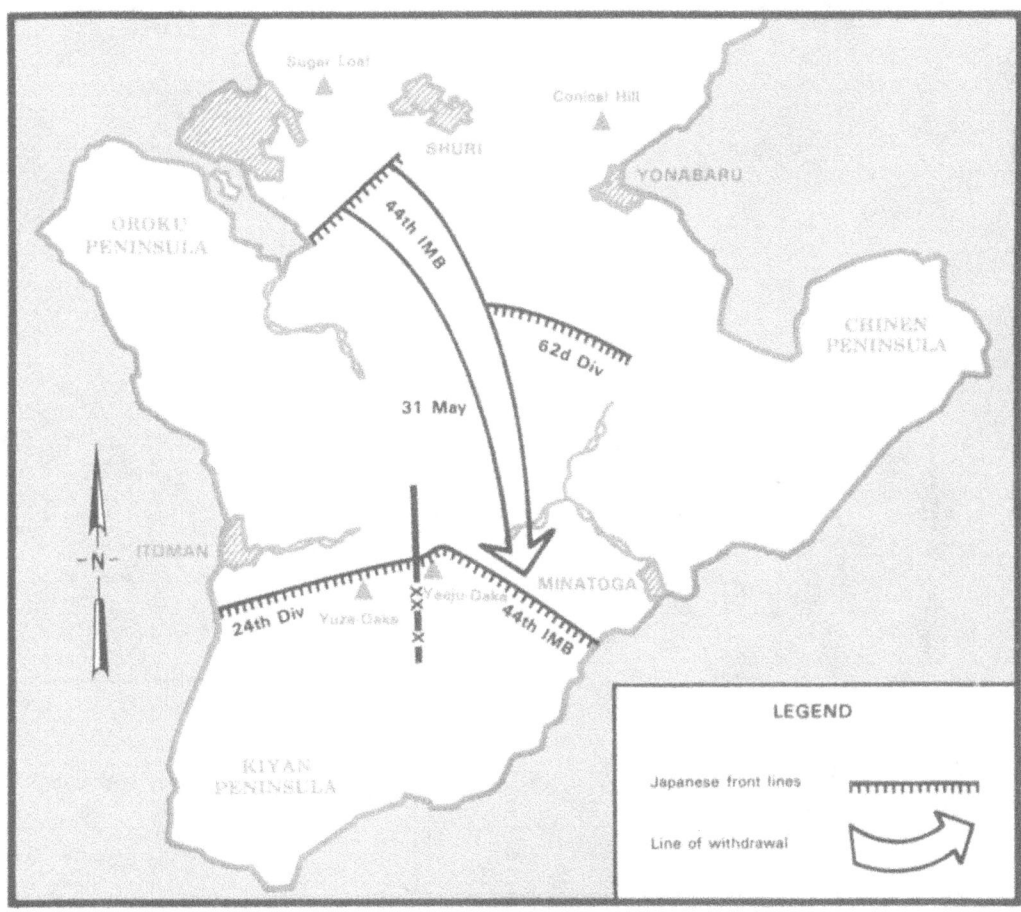

Map 11. Withdrawal of the 44th Independent Mixed Brigade, 31 May 1945

The withdrawal of 29 May to 4 June was completed in an orderly way, and the American forces did not inflict heavy losses by pursuit. These advantages were achieved by the retreat's being carefully planned and because the spring rainy season began in the last week of May, a little later and harder than usual. This hampered American tanks and reconnaissance aircraft. The rains also hampered the Japanese retreat transport, however, and turned the shafts of IJA caves into "small rivers." All of the Japanese movements were carried out under cover of darkness, and the 24th Transport Regiment of the 24th Division performed yeoman service with its eighty trucks.[42]

The Japanese withdrawal to fresh lines in the south succeeded in part because the Americans did not make an early concerted effort to break through the Shuri shell. On 26 May American aerial observers noted men, artillery, and armor moving south, but they also reported a large column moving north. This latter force was probably the IJA rear-area garrison units that were called up from the Chinen Peninsula to aid in the 25—26 May attacks on Yonabaru. Since the American analysts were not aware of

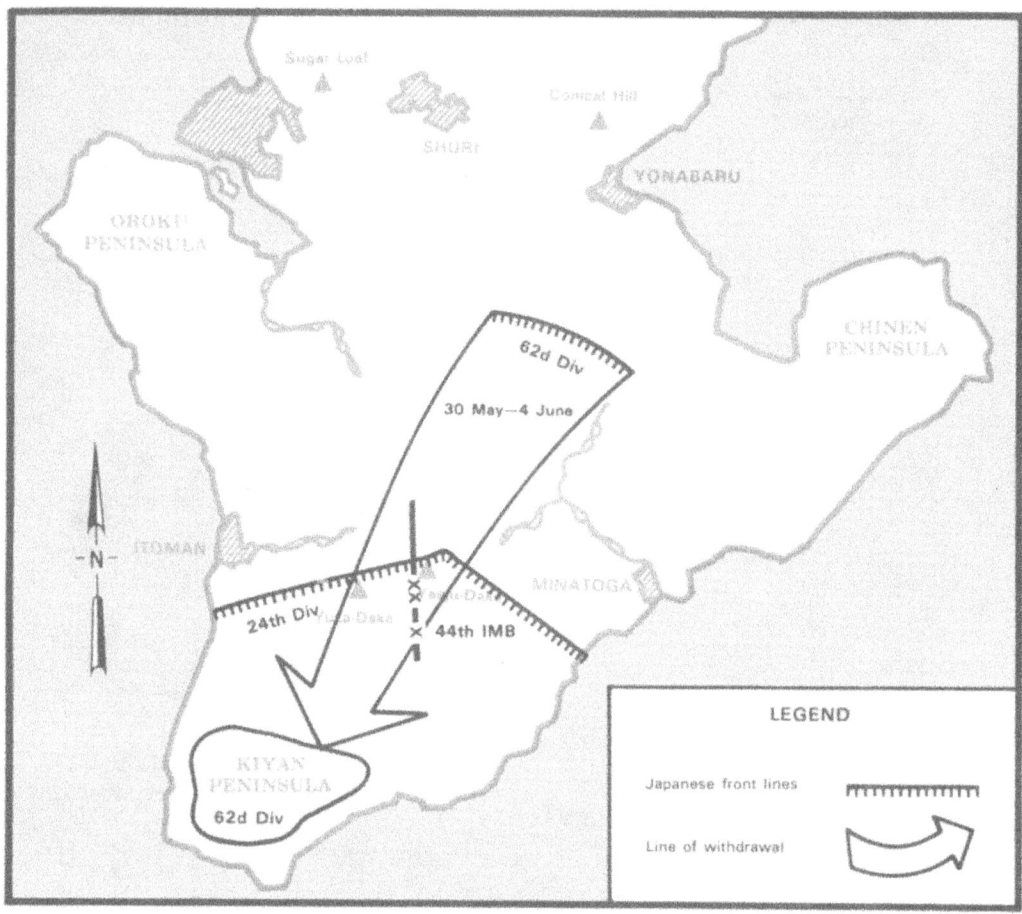

Map 12. Final withdrawal of the 62d Division, 4 June 1945

an overall pattern of southerly movement, they concluded that the Japanese were using the bad weather to cover an overdue rotation of reserve and frontline troops.[43]

Visibility on 29 May was zero, and air observation was impossible. Nevertheless, by 30 May, because of vacated IJA positions found west of Shuri and other accumulating bits of evidence, U.S. Tenth Army intelligence finally reached a consensus that the Shuri lines were being abandoned. But the Americans did not know where the new lines were and assumed they were about two miles behind the old ones, just enough to straighten out the salients the Americans had built up on the east and west.[44]

American forces elbowed into Shuri on 31 May, completing the reduction of the formidable Shuri line. They realized by this time that they were dealing only with a rear guard. The American force prepared to pursue the Japanese southward on 1 June, but by this time, the 44th IMB, the last IJA unit in the vicinity, had already completed its withdrawal. Moreover, given the sheltered nature of the Japanese defenses, it was impossible for the Americans to move forward safely if even a few Japanese remained in

A U.S. convoy in early June. Mud from spring rains hampered both the IJA withdrawal and the U.S. pursuit.

the pillbox caves. Those last few had to be eliminated, and that inevitably took days. The problem remained even after the Shuri line fell, because the IJA 62d Division and the 24th Division's rear guard both manned intermediate positions between Shuri and the Kiyan area. Even though the IJA screening forces were few, safe and rapid forward pursuit by the Americans was impossible. In the upshot, U.S. Tenth Army units were not aligned and ready to engage the new Kiyan lines until 6 June.[45]

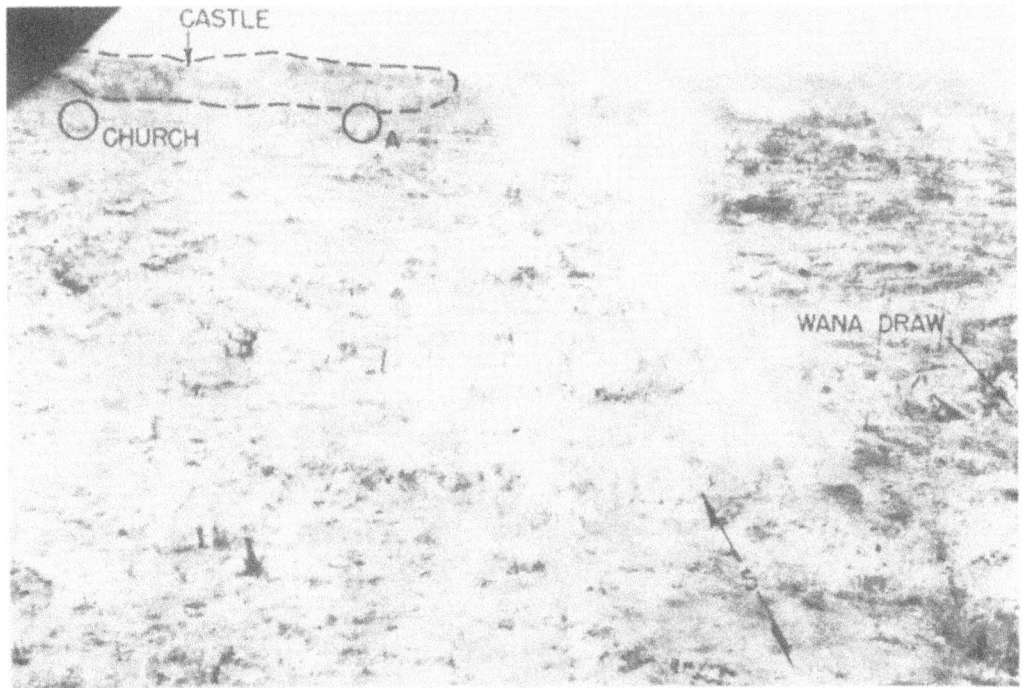

Shuri Ridge, site of the IJA 32d Army command cave (arrow), captured by U.S. forces on 31 May. Photograph of 23 May shows this area, formerly a town and fields, already rubbled by fire.

The Japanese thus succeeded in moving all their units intact to the south, and the Americans were unable to annihilate any through the rapid pursuit strategists dream of. Nonetheless, the IJA losses in the execution of this operation were staggering. When the 32d Army Staff took stock on 4 June of forces on hand, there were only 30,000 men left of the 50,000 men who had been present two weeks before. The 32d Army had lost 40 percent of its personnel in the one-week retreat, some through the 62d Division's aggressive attacks against the Americans at Yonabaru, some in the interdictive artillery fire directed at the Japanese on the roads, some in the countless, hopeless rear-guard defenses. Although historians have never made much of this, one must wonder if the smoothly executed retreat was really well advised or allowed the Japanese to resist for a longer period. Yahara, who condemned the heavy losses (7,000 men) of the 4 May offensive he opposed, had no self-criticism for the far heavier losses of the 29 May retreat that he sponsored.[46]

IJA staff officers noted that the 30,000 men who did survive now included few trained combat troops. Only 20 percent of the combat troops present on 1 April were still able to fight. Most of the personnel surviving after 4 June were service support and construction troops. Moreover, the retreat resulted in heavy losses of infantry weapons other than personal firearms. Only one-fifth of the machine guns and one-tenth of the heavier weapons survived. Hand grenades and mines were now almost exhausted. Only the large field guns that were kept in the rear with the 5th Artillery

Some troops and materiel were hit by interdictive fire in the 24 May—4 June retreat, including these IJA 150-mm howitzers

Command were relatively unscathed. Half of these were still intact, including sixteen 150-mm howitzers.[47]

Officers of the upper echelons also survived. Though company-grade officers serving in line companies were almost wiped out, battalion commanders and their staffs were nearly untouched. All but fourteen battalion-level staff members were still at their posts on 4 June. This allowed for maximum organizational cohesion in spite of the heavy losses on the line. Even so, these men were becoming increasingly exposed by the savage fighting, a staff without an army.[48]

The 32d Army on the Kiyan Peninsula was, in men and weapons, a diminished army, an army aware that its days of organized resistance were numbered. The army's final drama was played out in microcosm by the Okinawa Naval Base Force on Oroku Peninsula from 26 May to 13 June. The Naval Base Force, under Rear Admiral Ota Minoru, was positioned from the beginning of the campaign on Oroku Peninsula where it defended the naval port and air station. This force had developed elaborate seaward coastal defenses in cave emplacements and also land defense fortifications as other units had on Okinawa.

There were 8,825 IJN officers and sailors in the Naval Base Force as well as 1,100 Okinawan Home Guards, a total of 9,925 men. Of this total, however, only a few hundred had been initially trained and equipped for ground combat. All the rest were in signals, torpedo maintenance, naval stores, and the like. In short, the Oroku naval detachment, although it faced a seasoned ground combat force, was not one itself.[49]

On 26 May, as orders for the retreat to the Kiyan were being disseminated, the Naval Base Force received a radio message stating that it should destroy its heavy weapons and withdraw to the Kiyan Peninsula on 2 June. Ota misinterpreted the order, however, and moved his force to the Kiyan on 28 May. Almost immediately after reaching the new positions in the Kiyan, however, the naval force returned to its former base on Oroku without permission. Apparently, the Naval Base Force staff did not like the new positions and wished during its last stand to occupy the more familiar positions it had prepared and in that part of the island that had traditionally belonged to the navy. The 32d Army Staff, on hearing these sentiments expressed by Ota, was pleased to authorize the naval elements' return to the Oroku base after the fact, despite having just been ordered to leave it. The 32d Army accounts of this episode vary, but one may assume 32d Army was trying to alleviate its very serious faux pas of having ordered the Naval Base Force to die in army lines rather than defending its own base.[50]

The U.S. 6th Marine Division landed on Oroku's north coast on the morning of 4 June, and a pitched battle ensued that lasted ten days. The Okinawa Naval Base Force in the few days since its return to Oroku had resumed the defensive positions it had spent months preparing. The attacking U.S. Marines faced caves and sited machine-gun nets as they had on the Shuri line.

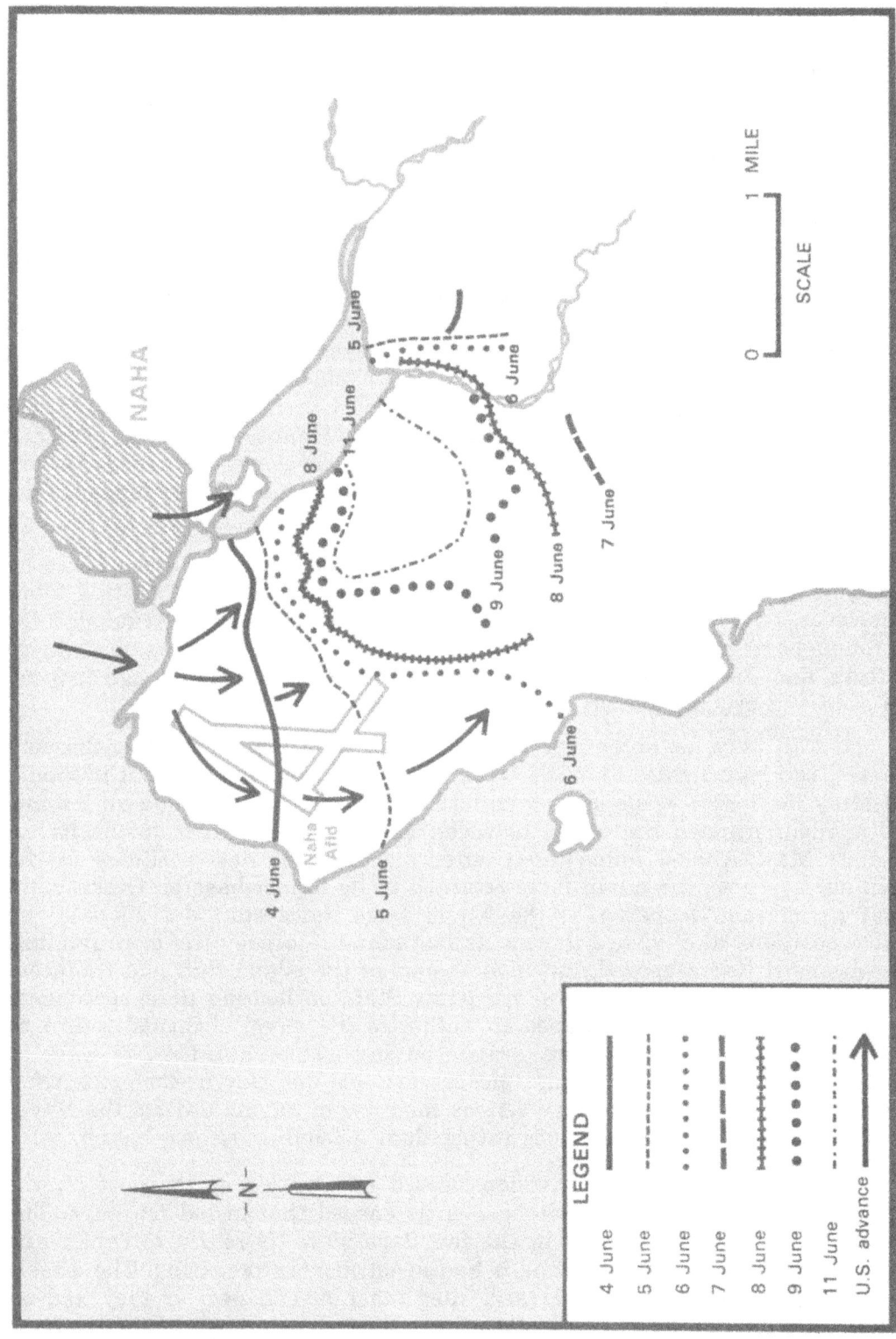

Map 13. The battle line on Oroku Peninsula, 4—13 June 1945

Although few of these IJN troops were trained for ground warfare, they were extremely resourceful in converting air and antiship equipment to ground use. The Japanese used 200-mm naval guns against tanks and fired 200-mm antiship rockets into the Marines' lines. The Marines called the rockets "locomotives from hell" because of the din, though, like the 320-mm mortars they had little fragmentation and caused few casualties. The Naval Base Force also used mines and mortars abundantly against the advancing Marines. Perhaps most effective, however, was its deployment of 252 machine guns, many of them taken from damaged aircraft. Even though this was a force not trained for ground combat, its resourcefulness and ample equipment allowed it to inflict casualties on the Americans at a rate comparable to that on the Shuri line.[51]

Even so, the U.S. 6th Marine Division pushed the Japanese Naval Base Force back down the peninsula and encircled it at the east end of the peninsula's base by 11 June (see map 13). Ota sent his farewell telegram to 32d Army on 11 June, and his headquarters sent its last message to 32d Army at 1600, 12 June. The IJN line broke on 12 June, and by 13 June organized resistance by the IJN had ceased. One hundred fifty-nine members of the Japanese Naval Base Force surrendered, the first time this occurred on Okinawa. Rear Admiral Ota Minoru and five of his aides committed suicide in the Oroku headquarters cave at 0100, 13 June.[52]

The Last Days, June 1945

The IJA's new Kiyan Peninsula line was largely in place by 3 June. The American forces had formed a line opposite it by 6 June and began their probing attacks on the east flank. The American forces did not reach the west part of the line until 9 June, being reluctant to move forward until the Oroku pocket was isolated, and did not attack in the west until 12 June, when the Oroku fighting had finished. The Americans had formed a continuous line, though the west end of the line did not approach the Japanese western positions until several days after contact had been made in the east. The Americans' advance was deliberate and cautious, so that they reached the Japanese line with the full benefit of their organization and firepower.[1]

The Japanese position was about five miles across and four miles deep. It was anchored along a line running from Kunishi Ridge in the west through Yuza-Dake and Yaeju-Dake peaks, to Hanagusuku village and Hill 95 on the east (see map 14). Manning this line from Kunishi to Yaeju-Dake were the 24th Division's 32d and 89th Regiments. The 24th Division set its headquarters at Medeera and held its 22d Regiment in reserve at nearby Makabe. Manning the line on the east, from Yaeju-Dake to the sea, were the 44th IMB's newly formed 6th Specially Established Regiment and the 15th Independent Mixed Regiment (IMR). The 44th IMB headquarters was placed above the coastal cliffs at Mabuni. Remnants of the 62d Division were held as a reserve at the southernmost tip of the peninsula. The 32d Army located its new headquarters at Mabuni near that of the 44th IMB.[2]

The arithmetic of units was now becoming crucial for the 32d Army Staff, because they were simply running out. The U.S. Infantry 7th Division pushed hard at the two ends of the 44th IMB position, at the Yaeju-Dake end and at the ridge running northeast from Hill 95. From 9 to 11 June, the Americans made a concerted attack against the center around Azato village and against Hill 95 on the east, resulting in their capture of Hill 95 on 11 June.[3]

On the night of 11—12 June, the 3d Battalion of the U.S. 17th Infantry Regiment accomplished a night infiltration that ejected the IJA 6th Special Regiment from the eastern foot of Yaeju-Dake. The 6th Specially Established Regiment was untried and had few combat soldiers in it. It had occupied

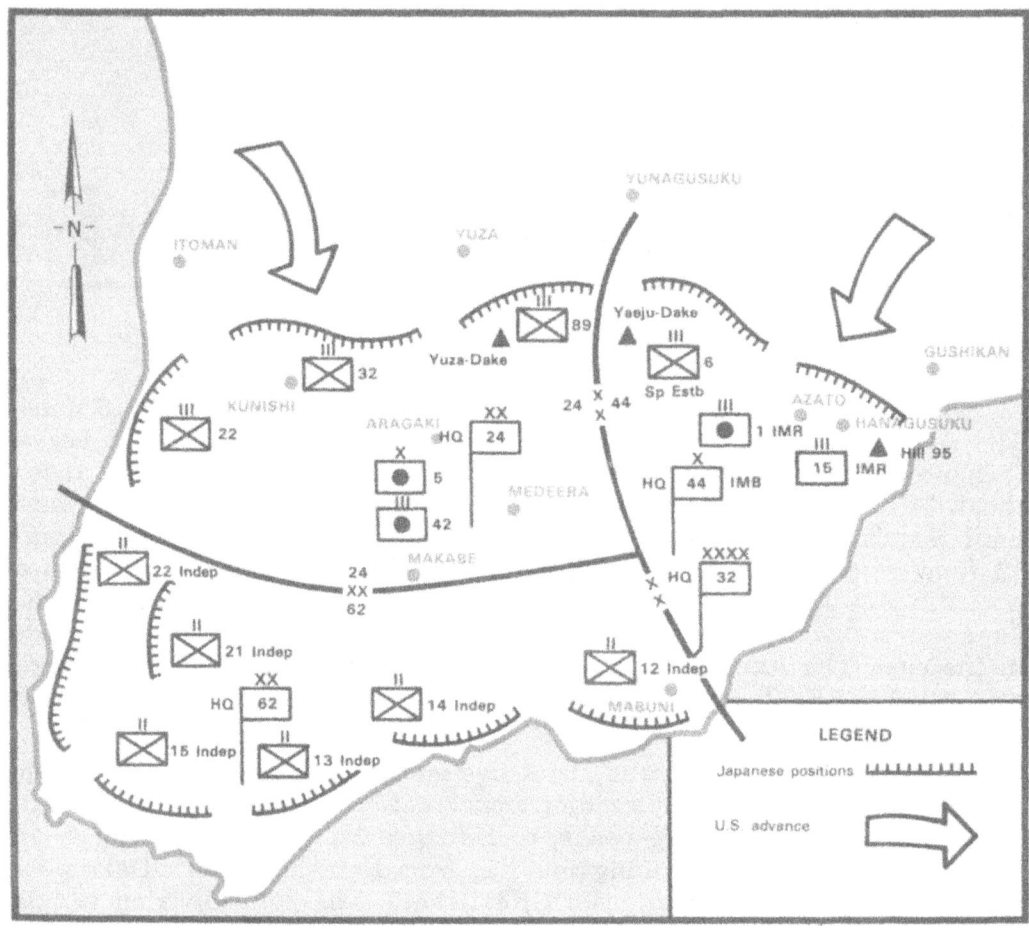

Map 14. The IJA Kiyan line, 4 June 1945

the eastern foot of Yaeju-Dake rather than the summit, as ordered, because it could obtain no water on the summit.[4]

By 12 June American forces had penetrated both flanks of the 44th IMB portion of the Kiyan line, thus threatening also the east flank of the 24th Division's part of the line. Under these circumstances, the 32d Army Staff hastened to send in its last reserves to stem the American advance. On 11 June, soon after the American attacks began in earnest on 9 June, the 32d Army Staff had already rushed some reinforcements to the critical Yaeju-Dake area. These were assorted small units, equal to about six companies, that 32d Army headquarters had on hand. They were drawn from the 5th Artillery units, a signal unit, and a field fortification unit. Unfortunately, because these troops were "equipped poorly as well as inadequately trained," they suffered heavy casualties on contact, and their efforts were "as ineffective as throwing water on parched soil."[5]

After the fall of Yaeju-Dake to the Americans on 12 June, the commander of the 24th Division made urgent pleas to 32d Army to recapture it

Yaeju-Dake as seen by approaching U.S. forces

Yaeju-Dake under U.S. preparatory fires

and so secure 24th Division's exposed right flank. Therefore, on 13 June, the 32d Army ordered the 15th Independent Infantry Battalion to drive the Americans out of the Yaeju-Dake area and the 13th Independent Infantry Battalion to attack the Americans on the extreme right, in the vicinity of Hill 95. Both of these battalions belonged to the 62d Division, the 32d Army's last reserve. These attacks, however, had almost no success. The 13th Independent Infantry Battalion promptly moved up to the line on the extreme right but lost more than half of its fighting strength on the first day. This was in part because the Americans had already taken Hill 95, leaving little terrain cover to the advancing 13th.[6]

The 15th Independent Infantry Battalion was not able even to reach the front expeditiously. The 24th Division commander protested the delay, and Operations Officer Yahara gave a direct order from the 32d Army to the 15th Independent Infantry Battalion commander to attack immediately. This kind of order, outside the chain of command, was almost unheard of. Even so, the 15th Independent Infantry Battalion was unable to advance. It encountered American tanks as it tried to move out of its reserve area toward Yaeju-Dake and did not have a single antitank gun. The commander, Major Iizuka, was himself wounded, and he commanded from a stretcher. The upshot was that the Americans secured their hold on Yaeju-Dake beyond retrieval.[7]

By 15 June, with both flanks already staved in, the 44th IMB's line was broken into fragments. Therefore, the 32d Army ordered the remainder of the 62d Division reserve force into the 44th IMB's zone. The 62d Division's commander, Lieutenant General Nakajima Gen, was given command of the 44th IMB as well as his own division. By 16 June the remainder of the 62d Division had made very slow progress toward the east, however, because of "unfamiliar terrain, darkness, and furious enemy shelling." Meanwhile, the extreme right flank unit of the 44th IMB, the 15th Independent Mixed Regiment, had lost contact with other units, and its headquarters was under attack by American tanks.[8]

By 17 June, the 44th IMB had fallen back to a new line running southeast from Yuza-Dake to the sea. This was held more thinly than the Yaeju-Dake—Hanagusuku line, but was at least a continuous line. The 62d Division intended to form a line behind this point, then advance to it. But the 62d Division had still made so little progress that it was ordered directly by 32d Army to advance its line as far as Mabuni, that is, up to within a half mile of where the 44th's line was. Only on 18 June was this movement accomplished. The 62d Division's 64th Infantry Brigade held the sector running from Yuza-Dake southeast to a point east of Medeera, and 63d Infantry Brigade held the sector running from a point east of Medeera to a point east of Mabuni and the sea.[9]

While the 44th IMB's front was being pushed back to Yuza-Dake—Mabuni on 6 to 18 June, the 24th Division's front was also hard-pressed. Because the Naval Base Force fighting on Oroku threatened the Americans' west flank, they were slower to probe forward on the west, the IJA 24th

Division's sector. By 11 June, however, the Americans had passed through all the rear guard resistance and had also subdued Oroku. They attacked the whole length of the 24th Division line, Kunishi—Yuza-Dake—Yaeju-Dake, on 12 June, after the east flank fighting had already been underway for six days.[10]

From 12 to 17 June, the IJA 24th Division's 32d and 89th Infantry Regiments sturdily held their ground against continuous attacks by the U.S. 1st Marine Division and part of the U.S. 96th Infantry Division. Here the Japanese resistance still had the quality it had had on the Shuri line. Relying on well-prepared caves and the high ground of Kunishi Ridge and Yuza-Dake, and having still a fair amount of trained manpower, the IJA 24th Division did not budge for five days, despite the usual bludgeoning by infantry-tank groups and fierce land, sea, and air saturation bombardment.[11]

The searing pattern of assault and counterassault typical of the Shuri fighting still appeared here. The U.S. Marines assaulted Yuza village for many days only to be driven out on as many nights. Before dawn on 12 June, two companies of the U.S. 7th Marine Regiment reached the crest of Kunishi Ridge itself, but at daylight, they were fiercely counterattacked and their communications cut off by the mortaring and shelling of the north face of the ridge they had just come up. Casualties in these isolated American companies were heavy, but they were nevertheless built up into a survivable fighting force in the next five days by the precarious expedient of handling all supply by tanks. Tanks brought reinforcements, plasma, and ammunition when they came up and carried out the wounded when they left. Any other movement across the deadly north slope area was impossible, because IJA 24th Division elements still held parts of the ridge and points east of the ridge so that they could carpet its whole face with fire. Things were no better for the Americans on the crest of the ridge. They could not stand up without being shot so that even the wounded had to be dragged on ponchos to the escape hatches under the tanks. The tanks themselves, which came up each day to fight for enlargement of the perimeter, were subject to 47-mm antitank fire on the road, both coming and going. Twenty-one American tanks were destroyed in the five days of Kunishi Ridge.[12]

The Japanese line east of Yaeju-Dake fell back a mile between 12 and 18 June, while the line west of Yaeju-Dake held rock steady. The reason for this discrepancy was that the east end of the line was engaged six days before the west end, but also lay in part in the west end's having a greater density of trained men and weapons than the east had. Thanks largely to a copious infusion of replacements from service support troops to the line divisions, the 24th Division on the west had 12,000 men, equal to 85 percent of its original strength. The east flank's 44th IMB had 3,000 troops, equal to 67 percent of its original numbers, while the 62d Division had 7,000, equal to about 60 percent of its initial roster.[13]

By 12 to 18 June, a majority of the units fighting east of Yaeju-Dake were already reorganized into rear-area units with few light weapons and almost no heavy ones. The 6th Specially Established Regiment, fighting on the 44th's left, for example, was a new reconstituted regiment, not a trained combat regiment, and was made up entirely of rear-area personnel. The same was true of the 62d Division's remnant that was sent to help the 44th. The 60 percent of the 62d's original strength level still on the line was not the 62d's original line combat component but everything else. As these forces went in on the Japanese right, they were "indignantly assaulting enemy tanks with clenched teeth and naked fists," as one reminiscing IJA staff officer put it. The problem east of Yaeju-Dake was not a problem of morale but simply a matter of the units there having reached the end of their resources, in numbers, weapons, and combat-trained leadership. This exhaustion of resources came a few days earlier on the IJA right than on the left because the Americans attacked sooner on the right and because the IJA units on the right were more battle worn.[14]

Some small efforts were made to solve the Japanese armaments problem between 12 and 17 June. Several planeloads of hand grenades and grenade launchers were parachuted in by the 6th Air Army. The untouched garrison on Tokuno Island sent five small boats of ammunition to the beleaguered 32d Army, but though they successfully negotiated the long sea voyage, they were sunk within sight of 32d Army's Kiyan position.[15]

By 18 June, the 24th Division's position on the Japanese left was also giving way. On 15 June, American units had penetrated an area between Yaeju-Dake and Yuza-Dake in the middle of the 89th Regiment's front. This led, on 19 June, to the death in combat of almost all officers and men of the 89th near Aragaki.[16]

The 22d Regiment was brought up from its rearward reserve position on 13 June, shortly after American attacks began in earnest on the 12th. To strengthen the far left of IJA 24th Division's sector, the American strength doubled in this area on 17 June when the U.S. 6th Marine Division, having finished at Oroku, took over the western half of the 1st Marine Division's line. At that time, the whole 22d Regiment line collapsed under the weight of the reinforced Marines' assault. The entire unit was overrun and wiped out. The regimental headquarters was surrounded, and almost all of its staff, including the commander, died in action.[17]

The 32d Regiment in the center still held out as of 17 June, even though its left flank, where the 22d Regiment had been, was completely unhinged. The U.S. Marines had already moved south through Maezato village by dusk of the 17th and were 1,000 yards in the left rear of the 32d Regiment's line. By 18 June, the 32d Regiment was fully enveloped on its left and rear, but its front remained intact. Meanwhile, the regimental headquarters was attacked from the rear by American infantry-tank groups. For four days, these attacks were fought back. By the evening of 22 June, however, the line battalions and the 32d's headquarters were separately enveloped and communications between them disrupted. Within a few days, the 32d Regiment, in its turn, had ceased to exist as a fighting force. By 22 June, nothing remained of the 24th Division except the division headquarters troops around Medeera and such refugees from the line regiments as had reached them.[18]

All of 24th Division, like the rest of the 32d Army on the Kiyan Peninsula, suffered from lack of combat personnel and arms. Combat ranks were badly thinned, so each regiment was reconstituted in the lull just after the arrival at the new Kiyan line. Medical, veterinary, supply, and other personnel were brought in to make good the losses. As a result, the line units consisted of men with a variety of specialties, none of which was combat.[19]

The Japanese shortage of weapons was telling. Men impressed from the rear had no weapons and were given none. Each reconstituted 24th Division battalion had to make do with eighty rifles, five light machine guns, and five grenade launchers. Even the machine-gun companies had only three to five machine guns, and regimental gun companies had only two guns. Moreover, not all of this scarce equipment was in good condition. Limited troop numbers, experience, and equipment all help to explain the abrupt dissolution of the 24th Division's line regiments between 17 and 22 June.[20]

By 19 June, it was apparent to the 32d Army Staff and its commander, Ushijima, that neither the west nor the east sectors of the army's line would hold. The staff therefore began doing some formal, but nevertheless important, things to prepare for the end of the army. On 10 June, a unit citation bearing Ushijima's signature had already been awarded to the 24th Division for its achievements on the Shuri line and in the 4 May offensive. Now, on 19 June, Ushijima's last order to the army congratulated all units on their performance. But, he noted, the army's weapons were nearly expended, and communications between units had been severed. Therefore, wherever communications were broken, the senior officer of any unit was authorized to command it without waiting on orders from a superior. All members of the army were to "fight to the last." Ushijima's last order made no mention of surrender.[21]

The 19 June order tidied up matters with respect to the subordinate units, but formalities toward superiors also had to be observed. On the evening of 18 June, Ushijima sent his farewell message to the vice chief of staff of the IJA, Kawanabe Torashiro, and to the commander of the 10th Area Army on Taiwan, Ando Rikichi. Ushijima ended his message with a poem: "May the island's green grass, which has withered waiting for autumn, be born again in the spring in our honored country."[22] This was reciprocated on 21 June when Army Minister Anami Korechika and Chief of the Army General Staff Umezu Yoshijiro sent their farewell messages back to the commander of 32d Army. Their coded radio transmissions also revealed that Lieutenant General Simon B. Buckner Jr., the U.S. Tenth Army commander, had been killed on 18 June. All of the 32d Army headquarters cheered at this news, beside themselves with joy. Only Ushijima grieved over the enemy commander's death and was much perplexed to find that his whole young staff was virtually rejoicing. Also on 20 June, the 32d Army received a dispatch from the 10th Area Army that contained a citation for all 32d Army.[23]

As Ushijima and Cho attended to these formal details, the two flanks of the U.S. forces continued to close southward like giant tongs around Medeera pocket as pivot. By 19 June, the U.S. Army XXIV Corps and U.S. III Amphibious Corps had pushed the IJA 44th IMB back to a line running from Medeera to Mabuni. On the west, the IJA 24th Division's line regiments had all been crushed or bypassed, so that the U.S. III Amphibious Corps was actually approaching Mabuni from the west. The American pincers were within two miles of closing, leaving only a narrow sliver of Okinawa in Japanese hands (see map 15). Outside this sliver, only a residual rear-area garrison force remained at the southernmost tip of the Kiyan Peninsula, which formed its perimeter north of Hill 72 and Uezato village. This small garrison group was isolated from major headquarters and would be overrun without great difficulty by the U.S. 6th Marine Division on 21 June.[24]

In fact, by 19 June the IJA sustained organized resistance only at two separated strongpoints, one around Mabuni, where the 32d Army headquarters had been located from early June and where the 62d Division headquarters and the remnant of the 44th IMB headquarters had now been driven. The other strongpoint was around Medeera where the 24th Division headquarters and troops attached to it still held a perimeter. By this time, all personnel—medical, technical, and other—were utilized as line combat troops.[25]

By 20 June, American forces closed the tongs, and only the Mabuni and Medeera strongpoints remained. The 32d Army Staff officers at Mabuni could hear fierce tank and small-arms battles in the intervals between bombardments. The struggle could be heard in every direction, less than a mile distant. The last contact between the 32d Army at Mabuni and the 24th Division at Medeera came by foot messenger on 20 June. At 1200 on 21 June, the small-arms firing in Mabuni village, 400 yards north of the headquarters cave, suddenly died away, which meant that the headquarters guard unit, sent forward to hold the village, had been wiped out. Within two hours, headquarters guards on Hill 89 overlooking one of the entrances of the headquarters cave were attacked by elements of the U.S. 7th Infantry Division and overrun. The Americans easily located the cave entrance shaft and dropped in explosives that killed ten officers and men of the staff. Despite all the casualties it had supervised since 1 April, these deaths on 21 June were the first battle injuries the 32d Army Staff had sustained in the whole campaign.[26]

These events meant that there were no longer any combat assets between the 32d Army Staff and its adversary. Even as late as 3 June, when two-thirds of 32d Army's complement had been lost, there had been almost no casualties at battalion level or above because line troops had sacrificially shielded the staffs. As of 22 June this had ceased to be the case. Nothing stood between the U.S. 7th Infantry Division and the commanders of 32d Army.

Since the 32d Army had ceased to be, planning its operations was a dead letter. Instead the 32d Army Staff, all that remained of the original

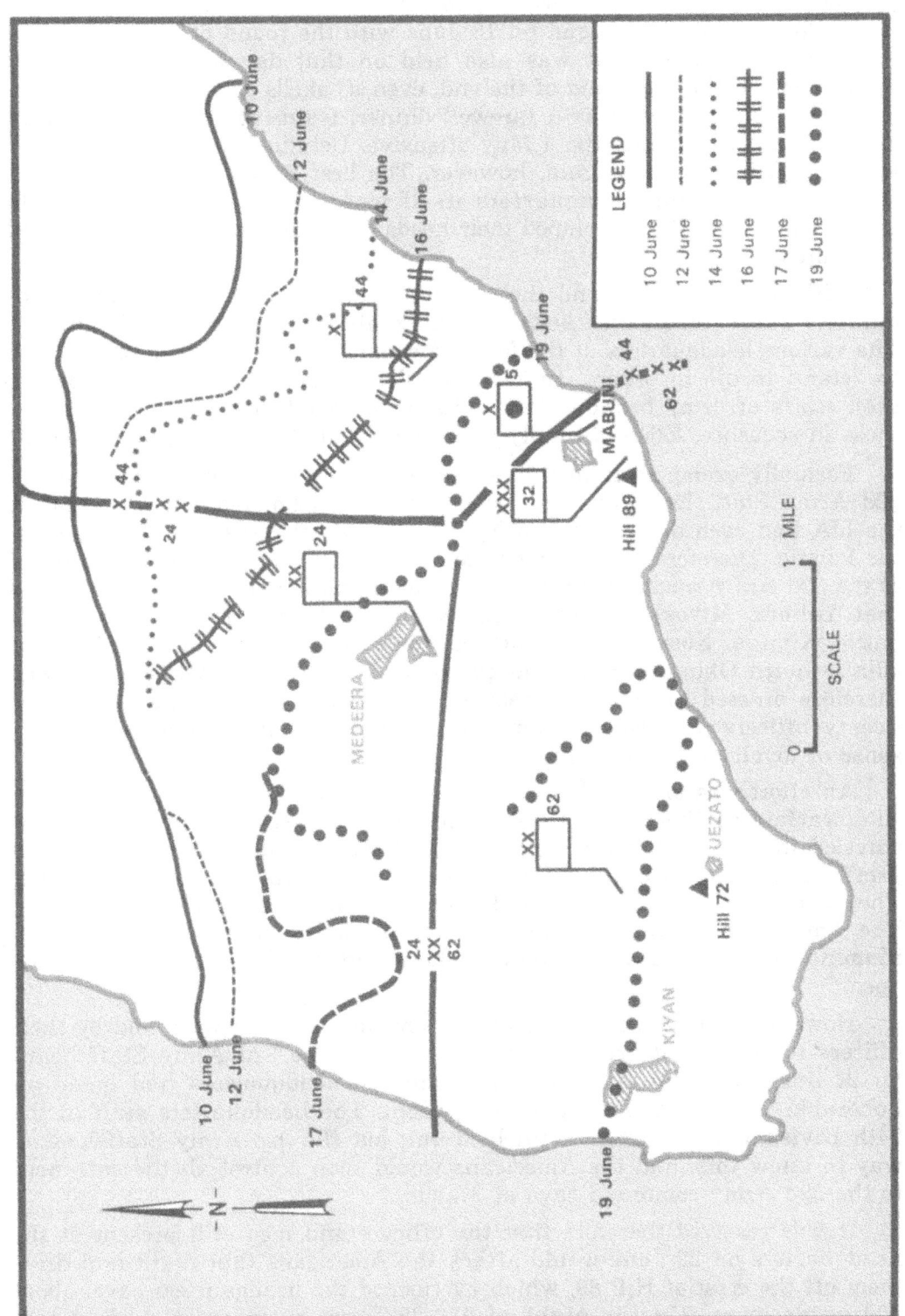

Map 15. Battle line on the Kiyan Peninsula, 10—19 June 1945

100,000-man organization, now had to attend to the orderly dissolution of itself. This process had begun on 18 June with the round of farewell orders and messages. A banquet was also held on that day for the 32d Army Staff, marking the beginning of the end, even as shells concussed the ground overhead. The banquet was a farewell dinner, featuring canned goods and sake, like that preceding the 4 May offensive. Ushijima and his entire staff were there. It was not a gala, however. The best Scotch had not survived the retreat, and the headquarters itself was only a natural cave little improved, where officers bumped their heads on stalactites and water dripped constantly.[27]

With farewell orders and the obligatory banquet out of the way, headquarters staffs themselves began to think about honorable death attacks. The various headquarters at the Mabuni command cave resolved on 21 June to "stand to die in order." In other words, brigade staffs, division staffs, then staffs of army headquarters units would conduct honorable death attacks in sequence, followed finally by suicide of the 32d Army commanders.[28]

Formally exempted from this expectation were the young officers of the 32d Army Staff, however. From the beginning, Cho had maintained that the IJA had been disadvantaged by the wanton self-destruction of staffs in the Pacific. Therefore, Cho decided, and ordered, that all of the staff officers of the 32d Army would avoid honorable death and ritual suicide. He specified that Yahara, Miyake, Nagano, and others would report to IGHQ on the battle. Kimura, Kusumaru, and others would escape from the Kiyan Peninsula to north Okinawa and wage guerrilla warfare. Each staff member was therefore ordered to make his escape on the night of 19 June, and about twenty officers and escort troops did. Even so, some remained out of a sense of loyalty to their commanders.[29]

An effort was also made to exfiltrate ordinary soldiers to carry on guerrilla warfare in the north. Troops sent north through the American lines traveled in groups of two or three, wore civilian clothes, and carried small arms only. A group usually carried only one firearm and some grenades. They moved on the night of 18—19 June and on several subsequent nights. The Americans, by this time accustomed to small-scale infiltration, put up illumination flares to detect these soldiers and killed most of them in the open.[30]

However, most of the troops at Mabuni and Medeera were told by their officers to continue to resist where they were. The 32d Army Staff heard on 21 June that the 5th Artillery Command headquarters had made an honorable death attack the preceding night. The headquarters staff of the 24th Division near Medeera still held out, but the 32d Army Staff had no way to know this, and the Americans would soon control all the entrances to the 32d Army command cave at Mabuni.[31]

It was resolved therefore that the officers and men still present at the headquarters on 22 June would attack the Americans that night and drive them off the crest of Hill 89, which overlooked the headquarters cave, about 400 yards away. On the night of 21—22 June, by moonlight, the headquarters guard unit did charge up the steep slopes toward the Americans, their last act. At this same time, in the respite thus guaranteed, Ushijima and Cho were to commit ritual suicide.³²

Hill 89. Last terrain feature defended under IJA 32d Army command

Ushijima's cook described what happened: At about 2200 on the night of 21—22 June, he was ordered to prepare an especially large dinner. He made it as sumptuous as he could, with rice, canned meats, potatoes, fried fish cakes, salmon, fresh cabbage, pineapples, tea, and sake. While the generals ate this feast, the cook immediately began making breakfast, as was customary, since no cooking smoke could be exposed after daylight. This saved his life, since the sentry at the cave entrance (whom the cook could see) and almost everyone else had been sent away to attack Hill 89 at 2330.³³

From his kitchen near the cave mouth, the cook was able to witness the generals' ritual suicides later that night. At about 0340, as the moon was just setting into the ocean, Ushijima and Cho went out of the cave onto the narrow ledges overlooking the sea. The ledges were too narrow for the generals to face north toward the imperial palace. Both Ushijima and Cho then committed *seppuku*, with their aides severing their heads instantly to minimize their suffering. Three orderlies secretly buried the bodies. Then, the remaining staff members obligingly went back into the cave to eat the breakfast the cook had prepared. That was the end of it. When night fell on 22 June, the cook fled, and the remaining staff sortied in their final "penetration attack" against the Americans who were, by now, in foxholes less than 100 feet away.³⁴

Ledges on Hill 89 where Ushijima and Cho committed ritual suicide

Only elements around the headquarters of the 24th Division at Medeera still fought on—but not for long. Only the 22d Regiment remained, and the 24th Division headquarters lost contact with it on 23 June. The 22d Regiment was overrun soon after. Somehow, the 24th Division headquarters managed to survive until 30 June, when its members also committed suicide in their command cave just south of Medeera.[35] This was an epilogue, however. Most observers describe the fighting as having substantially ended on 21 June.

Although the 32d Army had ceased to exist, some of its members still endured. Some lived passively but did not surrender, as Ito Koichi's men did in the same caves they had dug many months before. Also, remnants of the Kunigami Detachment still dwelled in the mountains in the far north.[36]

For the first time in the Pacific war, substantial numbers of IJA troops surrendered, 7,400 in all. Many, though, did not. Soldiers in the 32d Army were reluctant to surrender for several reasons: they were ordered not to surrender, and it was customary not to, but above all, their officers had told them and they believed that they would be tortured and killed if captured.[37]

Unfortunately, the prohibition against surrender left a large number of miserable and desperate IJA soldiers in open terrain. Sometimes, they committed suicide by stepping into a fire zone or by holding a grenade to their stomachs, a kind of "poor man's *seppuku*." Regrettably, during this period, many committed abusive acts against the civilian population. There were many cases in the Pacific war where Japanese soldiers carried out atrocities

Stunned IJA defender surrenders

A group of IJA 32d Army survivors after surrendering to U.S. forces

against subject peoples. Here, the atrocities were committed on a large scale against Japanese citizens. Knowing that death was imminent, the soldiers freely committed rape. In some cases, fearing discovery, the soldiers forced parents to kill their crying babies, or the soldiers killed the infants themselves. Sometimes, they killed Okinawans seeking to share a cave, fearing they were spies. This widespread abusiveness left deep scars and, to this day, is a divisive influence between the people of Japan and of Japan's Okinawa. For the average soldier, postbattle suicide was neither voluntary nor dignified. The no-surrender policy for the mass of soldiers was dehumanizing and had the unintended consequence of victimizing large numbers of Japanese civilians.[38]

Surviving civilians chatting with a U.S. soldier after the Okinawa battle

Japanese Casualties

IJA casualties are easy to calculate in the Okinawa campaign because there were only two kinds: POW and KIA (killed in action). The Japanese had 100,000 men on Okinawa, 67,000 IJA, 9,000 IJN, and 24,000 native Okinawans. Of these, 7,400 were taken prisoner and almost all the rest perished, the exception being the handful who surrendered after the war ended on 15 August. Many of the 7,400 captured were hastily impressed native Okinawans who were less imbued with the no-surrender doctrine.[39]

A total of 70,000 Japanese soldiers were lost by attrition in the first eight weeks of combat on the Okinawa isthmus. All of these were line combat soldiers and company-grade officers, leaving only the 32d Army's staffs and technical and rear-area personnel. The heavy artillery was still intact, but most of the infantry weapons were lost by the time of the 27 May—3 June retreat. The result after 3 June was that noncombat soldiers had to fight without weapons. These troops were simply overwhelmed. Whole lines melted away, and casualties in the third week of June skyrocketed, reaching 3,000 a day. For the first time on Okinawa, IJA soldiers went into the caves and cowered there for safety instead of using them as active fortifications.[40]

For the first time, Americans were able to roll from cave to cave with flamethrower tanks and explosives with little resistance between. American official histories tend to conceptualize this easy advance as a matter of anticave techniques being finally perfected, but the remaining Japanese' near-complete lack of weaponry and training may have been the operating factor. The IJN stand on Oroku, in contrast, though it also used inexperienced people, was rich in weapons, especially machine guns, and allowed no easy advance. American sources do not make much of the Japanese lack of weapons on Kiyan, perhaps feeling that even one machine gun in Japanese hands was one too many. Japanese officer observers all believed, however, that the shortage of small arms and antitank weapons was decisive for the poor quality of IJA fighting in the final weeks.

American Casualties

The secondary accounts of the Okinawa battle usually suggest that, against the Japanese combat losses of 100,000 dead or captured, the Americans suffered losses of only some 6,000. This indicates a highly favorable American loss ratio of 1 to 17. But the overall impact of Okinawa on American personnel was less positive than these triumphant figures suggest. Only 76,000 men in the Japanese force were uniformed and trained military; the other 24,000 persons were recently impressed indigenous militia and labor groups. Despite the IJA's sometime use of Okinawans in service roles, 76,000 is probably a more realistic figure for the real combat force U.S. divisions faced.[41]

To subdue these 76,000 IJA regulars cost U.S. Tenth Army exactly 6,319 KIA between 1 April and 30 June 1945. This figure is still one-twelfth of the Japanese number killed. What the figures conceal, however, is the substantial U.S. losses in categories other than KIA. The Tenth Army losses from 1 April to 30 June in WIA (wounded in action), IIA (injured in action), MIA (missing in action), and DOW (died of wounds) categories totaled 32,943 men, this in addition to the 6,319 KIA. Nor does the 6,319 figure include an additional 33,096 casualties in the "nonbattle" categories of sick, injured, other, and deaths. In other words, besides the KIA wastage, 66,039 Americans were lost to combat on account of wounds, illness, and death from various causes.[42]

Many of these recorded non-KIA casualties may have been minor, allowing them to return early to the fighting front. That such was not the case is suggested by the strength reports of the fighting divisions. As of 8 April, the present-for-duty strength of the four infantry and two Marine divisions, plus XXIV Corps and III Amphibious Corps service personnel, was 146,451. Added to these units' strength from 1 April to 30 June was a small but steady flow of replacements that totaled 22,801 men. The original force plus the replacements totaled 169,252 men. Nevertheless, the present-for-duty strength of the six divisions and two corps on 30 June was 101,462. This was an equation from which 67,790 American soldiers had disappeared. Of these, 6,319 were recorded KIA, leaving 61,471 other men still not capable of resuming their duties a week after the battle had ended. In other words, of the 66,039 non-KIA casualties, 61,471 were still serious enough that they had not reappeared for duty after the battle.[43]

It is likely that many of these 61,471 men would return to duty after weeks or months, after putting a proportionate strain on the medical system. Nevertheless, if all casualties are counted, not just KIA, the Americans' short- and medium-term loss from Okinawa operations totaled 72,358 men,* not too different from the total of IJA regulars present. American planners' anxieties about invading Japan proper may have sprung from this fact, known to them but not emphasized later, that the U.S. total casualty figure on Okinawa was 72,000 men.

Conclusion

The Japanese achievement on Okinawa was remarkable. Despite being outnumbered 2 to 1 in manpower and outgunned 10 to 1 in ground firepower alone, the Japanese mounted a dogged defense for ten weeks, denied their adversary strategically desired terrain, and inflicted casualties in all categories almost equal to their own numbers. Okinawa was the only occasion in the Pacific war, apart from Iwo Jima, where an IJA force acquitted itself so well. The credit for this achievement must go in part to staff decisions made long before the battle began. The building of the fire-port caves and the development of the doctrines for their use, as much as any other factors, allowed 32d Army to defeat the effect of the overwhelming land, air, and sea fires directed against it.

Although not usually thought of in these terms, the battle for Okinawa was a case where assiduous staff work overcame disproportionate firepower. Moreover, the Okinawa doctrinal solutions came mainly from the staff at the battle site, who to implement them, had to ignore both the IJA's deeply ingrained traditions of light infantry attack and the specific directives they received from higher headquarters. The staff members of the 32d Army were alone in their final responsibility for the outcome and also alone in the solutions they devised. Though none of the units present on Okinawa had served in earlier Pacific campaigns, the Okinawa staff did, to some extent, develop its doctrines in light of earlier combat events in the Pacific. Nonetheless, the 32d Army Staff members were successful mavericks who tempered their own operational doctrines in defiance of what they were advised to do by faraway theoreticians.

---

*6,319 KIA, 32,943 WIA and other battle casualties, and 33,096 nonbattle casualties.

The Okinawa battle was unusual in that it exhibited the stasis and lethality of World War I fronts even though it employed the full range of mobile World War II weapons: tanks, aircraft, radios, and trucks. On Okinawa, the modern weapons increased battle zone lethality due to bombardment and fire, without doing anything to decrease the static quality of the front. This suggests that dense battle, the "fire-swept zone" characteristic of World War I, may occur in modern warfare regardless of weaponry, wherever two large forces are concentrated to acquire the same finite objective. Episodes of dense battle therefore took place in World War II on Okinawa and Iwo Jima, as well as in the urban siege warfare of the several European fronts.

Dense battle makes special demands of an infantry force. Infantry on the surface in the fire-swept zone, whether attacking or counterattacking, must be fearless, agile, technically ingenious, and tolerant of heavy casualties. World War I staff officers invented a new kind of soldier that exemplified these qualities, the storm troops. Paradoxically, the old IJA doctrine's emphasis on fearless, almost thoughtless, light infantry attack was a suitable preparation for surface combat in the fire-swept zone. Light infantry combat, even hand-to-hand combat, flourished at the margins of the fire-swept zone, and in dense battle everything is done by margins. The IJA's old doctrines of boldness, extreme small-unit initiative, self-sacrifice, and close fighting were, unintentionally, an ideal training for dense battle in counterattack warfare, even though that training was antithetical to the larger operational doctrines needed on Okinawa.

The Okinawa infantry fighting, besides taking place in an environment of unusually high lethality, consisted on both sides of a main weapon—in caves or tanks—and the rifle teams protecting them. This pattern—the use of machine guns or machine-gun strongpoints—also emerged in the no-man's-land fighting of World War I. The Okinawa experience suggests that this tactical grouping may be one of the most basic in modern combat and likely to appear in a wide variety of circumstances and regardless of the specific configuration of the weapon. This means a modern operational planner must pay attention to both elements of the equation, the skilled infantry team and the weapon. On Okinawa, the U.S. Tenth Army won with tanks, and the IJA 32d Army defended as long as it did with sited fire ports that were low in technology but high in sophistication. Even so, both the caves and tanks were vulnerable unless protected by infantry, who ended in dueling at close ranges with small arms to decide the outcome.

Besides providing insights into modern infantry tactics, the Okinawa campaign demonstrates the transformation in defensive fortifications mandated by air power. The World War I trench erected a barrier toward the enemy in the front. But the advent of aircraft mandated a barrier against the enemy above. On Okinawa, the entire Japanese Army moved underground, lived underground, and performed most combat functions underground. This arrangement may prove a necessary feature of any future combat effort that does not enjoy air superiority. The IJA's operations on

Okinawa offer some helpful clues with respect to the effective use of such underground forts.

Finally, Japan's Okinawa experience demonstrates what resourceful and determined soldiers can do, even when facing superior numbers and simultaneous overwhelming lethality on land, air, and sea. Intelligence and diligence can stand against even the most extreme technological superiority. But not forever. Ultimately, brave men and overwhelming firepower will always defeat brave men alone.

Appendix A

32d Army Staff

Position	Incumbent
Commander	Lieutenant General Ushijima Mitsuru
Chief of staff	Lieutenant General Cho Isamu
Senior operations officer	Colonel Yahara Hiromichi
Army staff officer	Lieutenant Colonel Kimura Masaharu
Army staff officer	Major Jin Naomichi
Army staff officer	Major Miyake Tadao
Army staff officer	Major Kusumaru Kanenori
Army staff officer	Major Nagano Hideo
Senior deputy staff officer	Lieutenant Colonel Kuzuno Ryuichi
Weapons branch chief	Colonel Sakurai Mitsugi
Administration branch chief	Colonel Sato Miyoharu
Medical branch chief	Colonel Shinoda Shigeyoshi
Veterinary branch chief	Colonel Sato Takehisa
Legal affairs branch chief	Major Wada Kazuyoshi

Source: Okinawa Sakusen, Dai-niji sekai taisen-shi, Rikusenshi-shu 9, Rikusenshi kenkyu fukyukai ed. (Tokyo: Hara Shobo, 1968), 260.

Appendix B

IJA 32d Army Order of Battle, March 1945

Army Units

Unit	Strength
32d Army Troops	
Headquarters	1,070
Ordnance Depot	1,498
Ordnance Duty Unit	150
Field Freight Depot	1,167
36th Signal Regiment	1,912
Okinawa Army Hospital	204
27th Field Water Purification Unit	244
Well-Digging Unit	34
Defense Construction Unit	108
7th Fortress Construction Duty Company	322
2d Field Construction Duty Company	366
24th Infantry Division	
Headquarters	267
22d Infantry Regiment	2,796
32d Infantry Regiment	2,870
89th Infantry Regiment	2,809
42d Field Artillery Regiment	2,321
24th Reconnaissance Regiment	346
24th Engineer Regiment	777
24th Transport Regiment	1,158
Signal Unit	275
Decontamination Training Unit	77
Ordnance Repair Unit	57
Veterinary Hospital	11
Water Supply and Purification Unit	241
1st Field Hospital	174
2d Field Hospital	181

Unit	Strength
62d Infantry Division	
Headquarters	65
63d Brigade Headquarters	129
11th Independent Infantry Battalion	1,091
12th Independent Infantry Battalion	1,085
13th Independent Infantry Battalion	1,058
14th Independent Infantry Battalion	1,085
273d Independent Infantry Battalion	683
64th Brigade Headquarters	121
15th Independent Infantry Battalion	1,076
21st Independent Infantry Battalion	1,080
22d Independent Infantry Battalion	1,071
23d Independent Infantry Battalion	1,089
272d Independent Infantry Battalion	683
Engineer Unit	255
Signal Unit	359
Transport Unit	300
Field Hospital	371
Veterinary Hospital	22
44th Independent Mixed Brigade	
Headquarters	63
2d Infantry Unit	2,046
15th Independent Mixed Regiment	1,885
Artillery Unit	330
Engineer Unit	161
5th Artillery Command	
Headquarters	147
1st Medium Artillery Regiment (-)	856
23d Medium Artillery Regiment	1,143
7th Heavy Artillery Regiment	526
100th Independent Heavy Artillery Battalion	565
1st Independent Artillery Mortar Regiment (-)	613
1st Light Mortar Battalion	633
2d Light Mortar Battalion	615
21st Antiaircraft Artillery Command	
Headquarters	71
27th Independent Antiaircraft Artillery Battalion	505
70th Field Antiaircraft Artillery Battalion	513
80th Field Antiaircraft Artillery Battalion	517
81st Field Antiaircraft Artillery Battalion	514
103d Independent Machine Cannon Battalion	336
104th Independent Machine Cannon Battalion	338
105th Independent Machine Cannon Battalion	337

Unit	Strength
Machine-Gun Units	
3d Independent Machine-Gun Battalion	340
4th Independent Machine-Gun Battalion	344
14th Independent Machine-Gun Battalion	334
17th Independent Machine-Gun Battalion	331
Antitank Units	
3d Independent Antitank Battalion	363
7th Independent Antitank Battalion	353
22d Independent Antitank Battalion	402
32d Independent Antitank Company	144
11th Shipping Group	
Headquarters	100
7th Shipping Engineer Branch Depot	600
23d Shipping Engineer Regiment (-)	850
26th Shipping Engineer Regiment (-)	550
5th Sea Raiding Base Headquarters	42
1st Sea Raiding Squadron	104
2d Sea Raiding Squadron	104
3d Sea Raiding Squadron	104
26th Sea Raiding Squadron	104
27th Sea Raiding Squadron	104
28th Sea Raiding Squadron	104
29th Sea Raiding Squadron	104
1st Sea Raiding Base Battalion	886
2d Sea Raiding Base Battalion	874
3d Sea Raiding Base Battalion	877
26th Sea Raiding Base Battalion	908
27th Sea Raiding Base Battalion	897
28th Sea Raiding Base Battalion	900
29th Sea Raiding Base Battalion	900
49th Line of Communication Sector	
Headquarters	202
72d Land Duty Company	508
83d Land Duty Company	496
103d Sea Duty Company	711
104th Sea Duty Company	724
215th Independent Motor Transport Company	181
259th Independent Motor Transport Company	182
Engineer Units	
66th Independent Engineer Battalion	865
14th Field Well Drilling Company	110
20th Field Well Drilling Company	110

Unit	Strength
19th Air Sector Command	
Headquarters	41
29th Field Airfield Construction Battalion	750
44th Airfield Battalion	377
50th Airfield Battalion	360
56th Airfield Battalion	380
3d Independent Maintenance Unit	120
Makoto 1st Maintenance Company	90
118th Independent Maintenance Unit	100
6th Fortress Construction Duty Company	330
Detachment, 20th Air Regiment	27
10th Field Meteorological Unit	80
26th Air-Ground Radio Unit	117
46th Independent Air Company	132
1st Branch Depot, 5th Field Air Repair Depot	130
21st Air Signal Unit	310
Okinawa Branch, Army Air Route Department	359
223d Specially Established Garrison Company	200
224th Specially Established Garrison Company	200
225th Specially Established Garrison Company	200
27th Tank Regiment	750
Army Unit Total	66,636[a]

Navy Units

Unit	Strength
Okinawa Base Force (Headquarters, Coast Defense, and Antiaircraft Personnel)	3,400
27th Motor Torpedo Boat Squadron	200
33d Midget Submarine Unit	130
37th Torpedo Maintenance Unit	140
Torpedo Working Unit	130
81-mm Mortar Battery	150
Oroku Transmitting Station	30
Naha Branch, Sasebo Naval Stores Department	136
Naha Branch, Sasebo Transportation Department	136
Naha Navy Yard, Sasebo Naval Base	53
Oroku Detachment, 951st Air Group	600

[a] This figure represents the total Japanese strength. Included in it, however, are an estimated 5,000 Okinawans, mostly regular conscripts, who were integrated into Japanese units.

Unit	Strength
Nansei Shoto Air Group	2,000
226th Construction Unit	1,420
3210th Construction Unit	300
Navy Unit Total	8,825[b]

Okinawan

502d Special Guard Engineer Unit	900
503d Special Guard Engineer Unit	700
504th Special Guard Engineer Unit	700
Blood-and-Iron-for-the-Emperor Duty Unit	750
Boeitai Assigned to the Army	16,600
Boeitai Assigned to the Navy	1,100
Students	600
Regular Conscripts Not Included Under Army Units	2,000
Okinawan Total	23,350
Grand Total (Rounded Out)	
Army Units	67,000
Navy Units	9,000
Okinawans	24,000
Japanese Strength on Okinawa	100,000[c]

[b]This total represents both regular naval ratings and the Japanese, Korean, and Okinawan military civilians who were utilized in the naval land combat organization.

[c]Strength figures have been rounded.

Source: Charles S. Nichols and Henry I. Shaw, *Okinawa: Victory in the Pacific* (Washington, DC: Historical Branch, G-3 Division, U.S. Marine Corps, 1955), 302—4.

Notes

Chapter 1

1. Boei kenkyujo senshishitsu, ed., *Okinawa homen rikugun sakusen, Senshi sosho*, vol. 11, [Okinawa area infantry strategy, War History Series] (Tokyo: Asakumo shimbunsha, 1968), 2—3, hereafter cited as *OHRS*; and U.S. Army Forces Far East, Military History Section, ed., Japanese Monograph no. 135, *Okinawa Operations Record* (Washington, DC, 1949), Book 1, "Okinawa Operations Record of 32d Army," 1, hereafter cited as JM 135.

2. JM 135, 2—3.

3. Inagaki Takeshi, *Okinawa: higu no sakusen* [Okinawa: A strategy of tragedy] (Tokyo: Shinchosha, 1984), 85.

4. JM 135, 4.

5. U.S. Army, 77th Infantry Division, G-2 Section, "G-2 Summary—Okinawa From 27 April 1945 to 10 June 1945" (Okinawa, June 1945), 17, hereafter cited as 77th ID, "G-2 Summary."

6. Inagaki, *Okinawa*, 86.

7. JM 135, 9—10.

8. Ibid., 18—19.

9. Ibid., 11.

10. Ibid., 20-20B, 20D-20G.

11. Inagaki, *Okinawa*, 108.

12. *OHRS*, 132—35; and Inagaki, *Okinawa*, 109—11, 116.

13. JM 135, 30; *OHRS*, 135—36; and Inagaki, *Okinawa*, 118.

14. *OHRS*, 136; and Inagaki, *Okinawa*, 118—19.

15. *OHRS*, 136—37; and Inagaki, *Okinawa*, 119—20.

16. JM 135, 28B, 29; and *OHRS*, 137.

17. Ibid.

18. JM 135, 29—30.

19. Inagaki, *Okinawa*, 122.

20. *OHRS*, 168—70; Inagaki, *Okinawa*, 133—34; and JM 135, 32.

21. *OHRS*, 167—68; Inagaki, *Okinawa*, 134, 136.

22. Inagaki, *Okinawa*, 138—39.

23. Ibid., 139—40.

24. Ibid., 140.
25. Ibid.
26. JM 135, 50—51; and Inagaki, *Okinawa*, 142.
27. JM 135, 49; and Inagaki, *Okinawa*, 142.
28. JM 135, 49—50.
29. Ibid., 50.
30. Roy E. Appleman, et al., *Okinawa: The Last Battle*, U.S. Army in World War II (1948; reprint, Washington, DC: Department of the Army, 1971), 9; and JM 135, 56—57.
31. Charles S. Nichols and Henry I. Shaw, *Okinawa: Victory in the Pacific* (Washington, DC: Historical Branch, G-3 Division, U.S. Marine Corps, 1955), 57, 303—4; and JM 135, 40—41.
32. *OHRS*, 622—24; and JM 135, 41—42.
33. JM 135, 57.
34. Nichols and Shaw, *Okinawa*, 302—4.
35. Ibid., 302; *OHRS*, Enclosed chart 2; and Inagaki, *Okinawa*, 94.
36. Morimatsu Toshio (former captain IJA), interview with author, Tokyo, Japan, November 1985; Nichols and Shaw, *Okinawa*, 50, 57; and *OHRS*, Enclosed chart 2.
37. Nichols and Shaw, *Okinawa*, 50, 58; and *OHRS*, Enclosed chart 2.
38. Morimatsu interview; and Nichols and Shaw, *Okinawa*, 50.
39. *OHRS*, Enclosed charts 1 and 2; and Nichols and Shaw, *Okinawa*, 56.
40. Nichols and Shaw, *Okinawa*, 51—52, 302.
41. Inagaki, 95.
42. *OHRS*, Enclosed chart 2.
43. Nichols and Shaw, *Okinawa*, 51, 303; and *OHRS*, Enclosed chart 2.
44. Nichols and Shaw, *Okinawa*, 303.
45. Ibid., 53, 303.
46. Ibid., 302—3.
47. JM 135, 37; Nichols and Shaw, *Okinawa*, 57—58; and *OHRS*, 174—75.
48. JM 135, 38; Nichols and Shaw, *Okinawa*, 58, 303; and *OHRS*, 176.
49. JM 135, 39; Nichols and Shaw, *Okinawa*, 58, 303; and *OHRS*, 176.
50. Ibid.
51. JM 135, 40.
52. Nichols and Shaw, *Okinawa*, 58—59.
53. *OHRS*, Enclosed chart 1.
54. Inagaki, *Okinawa*, 94; *OHRS*, 635; and James Belote and William Belote, *Typhoon of Steel: The Battle for Okinawa* (New York: Harper and Row, 1970), 18.
55. Inagaki, *Okinawa*, 91; Belote, *Typhoon*, 18; and *OHRS*, 52, 635, and Enclosed chart 1.
56. Inagaki, *Okinawa*, 91—92; Belote, *Typhoon*, 18; and *OHRS*, 52, 635, and Enclosed chart 1.

57. Inagaki, *Okinawa*, 92.

58. *OHRS*, 635—36.

59. JM 135, 45—46; and *OHRS*, 188—89.

60. JM 135, 2, 19; and Inagaki, *Okinawa*, 87, 89.

61. *OHRS*, 96—103; and Inagaki, *Okinawa*, 97—98.

62. Inagaki, *Okinawa*, 149; and JM 135, 29.

63. Inagaki, *Okinawa*, 151—52; and *OHRS*, 188.

Chapter 2

1. JM 135, 61.

2. Jeter A. Isely and Philip A. Crowl, *The U.S. Marines and Amphibious War: Its Theory and Practice in the Pacific* (Princeton, NJ: Princeton University Press, 1951), 556; and JM 135, 63—64.

3. Inagaki, *Okinawa*, 154—55.

4. Isely and Crowl, *U.S. Marines*, 55.

5. JM 135, 68—69; and *OHRS*, 269.

6. John H. Bradley, *The Second World War: Asia and the Pacific*, West Point Military History Series (Wayne, NJ: Avery Publishing, 1984), 68; and Nichols and Shaw, *Okinawa*, 56.

7. Inagaki, *Okinawa*, 163; and JM 135, 70.

8. Ibid.

9. Inagaki, *Okinawa*, 164—65; and JM 135, 70.

10. Inagaki, *Okinawa*, 165, 167.

11. Ibid., 168.

12. Ibid., 169; and JM 135, 71.

13. Inagaki, *Okinawa*, 169; and JM 135, 72—76.

14. Inagaki, *Okinawa*, 169; and JM 135, 78.

15. Inagaki, *Okinawa*, 175—76.

16. *OHRS*, Enclosed maps 4, 5; and Appleman, *Okinawa*, Enclosed maps 5, 7.

17. *OHRS*, Enclosed map 4; and Appleman, *Okinawa*, Enclosed map 14.

18. JM 135, 81—82.

19. Ibid., 82—83.

20. Ibid., 83.

21. Ibid., 83—84.

22. Ibid., 84—85.

23. Inagaki, *Okinawa*, 178.

24. Ibid., 178—79.

25. Mikami Masahiro, "62d Division Crisis and Commitment of the Bulk of 32d Army in the Northern Front," in *Okinawa Campaign, Data for MHX-85*, translated by Yanase Tokui (Tokyo: JGSDF Staff College, December 1985), 45—47.

26. Appleman, *Okinawa*, Enclosed map 23.

27. Yahara Hiromichi, *Okinawa kessen* [Battle of Okinawa] (Tokyo: Yomiuri shimbunsha, 1972), 225; and Mikami, "62d Division Crisis," Appendix 3, 67.

28. Nichols and Shaw, *Okinawa*, 126.

29. Mikami, "62d Division Crisis," 52; and Yahara, *Okinawa*, 225 ff.

30. Mikami, "62d Division Crisis," 52—53; and Yahara, *Okinawa*, 225 ff.

31. Mikami, "62d Division Crisis," 53; and Inagaki, *Okinawa*, 191.

32. See Mikami, "62d Division Crisis," 54, and Appendix 7, 71; and JM 135, 94—95.

33. Appleman, *Okinawa*, 258—59.

34. Ibid., 258—59.

35. Ibid., 260, 262—63.

Chapter 3

1. U.S. Army, 10th Army, G-2, *Intelligence Monograph, Ryukyus Campaign* (Okinawa, 1945), pt. II, sect. D, 1, hereafter cited as 10th Army, *Monograph*.

2. Ibid., 3—5.

3. Ibid., 4, 6—12.

4. Ibid., 4, 8, 10; and Inagaki, *Okinawa*, 180.

5. 10th Army, *Monograph*, pt. II, sect. D, 40; and Inagaki, *Okinawa*, 180—81.

6. Inagaki, *Okinawa*, 180.

7. 10th Army, *Monograph*, pt. I, sect. A, 5.

8. Appleman, *Okinawa*, 250; and 10th Army, *Monograph*, pt. I, sect. C, chap. II, 7, and pt. I, sect. D, chap. III, 23.

9. 10th Army, *Monograph*, pt. I, sect. D, chap. III, 24, and pt. II, sect. A, 35.

10. Inagaki, *Okinawa*, 141.

11. 10th Army, *Monograph*, pt. II, sect. B, 4—5.

12. Ibid., 8.

13. Ibid., pt. II, sect. B, 5, 6, 8, and pt. II, sect. C, 9.

14. Appleman, *Okinawa*, 249.

15. Inagaki, *Okinawa*, 186.

16. Ibid.

17. Appleman, *Okinawa*, 249.

18. 10th Army, *Monograph*, pt. II, sect. C, 2—3, and pt. I, sect. D, chap I, 8.

19. Ibid., pt. II, sect. A, 20—21, 35, and pt. II, sect. B, 8—9.

20. Eric J. Leed, *No Man's Land: Combat and Identity in World War I* (London: Cambridge University Press, 1979), 130, 139—40.

21. Appleman, *Okinawa*, 10; and 10th Army, *Monograph*, pt. I, sect. A, 4.

22. U.S. Army, 10th Army, G-2 Section, "G-2 Weekly Summary, Number 2" (Okinawa, 4 June 1945), Annex C, Inclosure 5, 1, hereafter cited as 10th Army, "G-2 Summary."

23. Inagaki, *Okinawa*, 185.

24. Ibid.; and Appleman, *Okinawa*, 256.

25. U.S. Army, 10th Army, G-1 Section, "G-1 Periodic Reports," Numbers 1 to 14 (Okinawa, 1 April 1945—7 July 1945), hereafter cited as 10th Army, "G-1 Periodic Reports."

26. See, for example, Appleman, *Okinawa*, 250—54.

27. Inagaki, *Okinawa*, 183.

28. U.S. Army Ground Forces, G-2 Section, "Information on Japanese Defensive Installations and Tactics" (Washington, DC, August 1945), section titled "Japanese Combat Methods on Okinawa," 2, hereafter cited as AGF, "Japanese Defensive Installations."

29. Appleman, *Okinawa*, 256.

30. AGF, "Japanese Defensive Installations," Inclosure no. 7, "32d Army Combat Directive No. 13," 5.

31. U.S. War Department, TM-E 30—480, *Handbook on Japanese Military Forces* (Washington, DC, 1 October 1944), 218.

32. 10th Army, "G-2 Summary," 1.

33. AGF, "Japanese Defensive Installations," Inclosure no. 7, "32d Army Combat Directive No. 13," 7.

34. 77th ID, "G-2 Summary," 15; and U.S. Army, 77th Infantry Division, G-2 Section, "G-2 Periodic Report [Daily]" (Okinawa, 25 May 1945), 4.

35. Ito Koichi (former captain, IJA), interview with author, Tokyo, Japan, 28 November 1985.

36. U.S. Army Forces, Pacific Ocean Areas, Assistant Chief of Staff, G-2 Section, "Test of Japanese Demolitions, Technical Intelligence Bulletin No. 16" (Guam, June 1945), 1—23; U.S. War Department, Military Intelligence Division, *Japanese Tank and Antitank Warfare* (Washington, DC, 1945), 213—25; and 77th ID, "G-2 Periodic Report," 25 May 1945, 4.

37. Ito interview; 77th ID, "G-2 Summary," 15; and 77th ID, "G-2 Periodic Report," 22 June 1945, 4.

38. See Alvin D. Coox, *Nomonhan: Japan Against Russia, 1939*, 2 vols. (Stanford, CA: Stanford University Press, 1985), 2:1,000—32.

39. U.S. Marine Corps, 6th Marine Division, "Sixth Marine Division on Okinawa Shima, G-2 Summary" (Okinawa, August 1945), 5, hereafter cited as 6th Mar. Div., "G-2 Summary"; and 77th ID, "G-2 Periodic Report," 25 May 1945, 4.

40. 6th Mar. Div., "G-2 Summary," 5, 8.

41. AGF, "Japanese Defensive Installations," section titled "Japanese Combat Methods on Okinawa," 2; Appleman, *Okinawa*, 255—56; Inagaki, *Okinawa*, 188; and 77th ID, "G-2 Periodic Report," 25 May 1945, 4.

42. Ibid.; and U.S. Commander in Chief, Pacific, and Commander in Chief, Pacific Ocean Areas, "Searching Caves: A Summary of Techniques Developed at Okinawa, CINCPAC-CINCPOA Bulletin No. 189-45" (Guam, August 1945).

43. 6th Mar. Div., "G-2 Summary," 8; and Ito interview.

44. Inagaki, *Okinawa*, 143; Nichols and Shaw, *Okinawa*, 302; and JM 135, 20B-20C.

45. 10th Army, *Monograph*, pt. I, sect. D, chap. I, 27; and Inagaki, *Okinawa*, 143.

46. Inagaki, *Okinawa*, 183; Appleman, *Okinawa*, 91; and 77th ID, "G-2 Summary," 15.

47. 10th Army, *Monograph*, pt. I, sect. D, chap. I, 1—27.

48. Ibid., 11.

49. Ibid., pt. I, sect. D, chap. II, 1—19; and 6th Mar. Div., "G-2 Summary," 44—45.

50. 10th Army, *Monograph*, pt. I, sect. D, chap. I, 3.

51. 77th ID, "G-2 Summary," 14; and Yahara, *Okinawa*, 192.

52. Appleman, *Okinawa*, 257; and 77th ID, "G-2 Summary," 14.

53. 77th ID, "G-2 Summary," 14.

54. 10th Army, *Monograph*, pt. I, sect. D, chap. I, 2, 17.

55. Ibid., 2, 3; and Inagaki, *Okinawa*, 144.

Chapter 4

1. Yahara, *Okinawa*, 234—36.

2. Inagaki, *Okinawa*, 194; and JM 135, 98.

3. JM 135, 97—99.

4. Inagaki, *Okinawa*, 194—95.

5. Yahara, *Okinawa*, 236—37; and Inagaki, *Okinawa*, 195.

6. Yahara, *Okinawa*, 238; and Inagaki, *Okinawa*, 196.

7. Yahara, *Okinawa*, 235.

8. Nishimura Hitoshi, "Command and Staff Activities in the Offensive Operations on 4 May 1945," in *Okinawa Campaign, Data for MHX-85*, translated by Yanese Tokui (Tokyo: JGSDF Staff College, December 1985), 91—94.

9. Yahara, *Okinawa*, 237—39.

10. Ibid.

11. Inagaki, *Okinawa*, 197; and Nishimura, "Command," 97—99.

12. Yahara, *Okinawa*, 243—44.

13. JM 135, 103, 106.

14. JM 135, 104.

15. Yahara, *Okinawa*, 247; and JM 135, 105.

16. Appleman, *Okinawa*, 289—91; and JM 135, 104.

17. JM 135, 104.

18. Yahara, *Okinawa*, 248—49.

19. Ibid., 251; and Ito interview.

20. Ito interview.

21. Yahara, *Okinawa*, 252; JM 135, 105, 108; and Appleman, *Okinawa*, 302.

22. Appleman, *Okinawa*, 287, 289.

23. Ibid.

24. JM 135, 107—8.

25. Yahara, *Okinawa*, 250; and Inagaki, *Okinawa*, 198.

26. Appleman, *Okinawa*, 299—301; Yahara, *Okinawa*, 251; Ito interview; and Inagaki, *Okinawa*, 199.

27. Nishimura, "Command," 88; and Inagaki, *Okinawa*, 199—200.

28. Rikusen-shi kenkyu fukyu kai, ed. [Land Warfare Research and Publicization Association, ed.] *Okinawa sakusen, Dainiji sekai taisen shi, Rikusen shishu 9* [Okinawa strategy, history of World War II, land warfare history collection, vol. 9] (Tokyo: Hara shobo, 1974 [1968]), 198; and Nishimura, "Command," 112.

29. Yahara, *Okinawa*, 262—63; and Inagaki, *Okinawa*, 215.

30. Yahara, *Okinawa*, 264.

31. Appleman, *Okinawa*, 311—23, Enclosed map 35.

32. Inagaki, *Okinawa*, 207—8

33. JM 135, 116.

34. Ibid., 117.

35. Ibid., 118.

36. Yahara, *Okinawa*, 292.

37. Ibid.

38. Ibid., 293.

39. Yahara, *Okinawa*, 294; and JM 135, 119.

40. JM 135, 123, 126; and Appleman, *Okinawa*, Enclosed map 44.

41. JM 135, 122—24.

42. Yahara, *Okinawa*, 303; JM 135, 125; and Appleman, *Okinawa*, 392.

43. Appleman, *Okinawa*, 389, 391.

44. Ibid., 392.

45. Ibid., 396—400, 424—27, 434—39.

46. JM 135, 130.

47. Ibid., 130—32.

48. Ibid., 130—31.

49. Nichols and Shaw, *Okinawa*, 303; and *OHRS*, 569.

50. Inagaki, *Okinawa*, 214; Appleman, *Okinawa*, 428; and JM 135, 127.

51. Nichols and Shaw, *Okinawa*, 218—19, 228; and *OHRS*, 569.

52. Nichols and Shaw, *Okinawa*, 227, Enclosed map 36; Appleman, *Okinawa*, 433; and *OHRS*, 579.

Chapter 5

1. JM 135, 134—35; and *OHRS*, Enclosed map 5.
2. JM 135, 132A.
3. Appleman, *Okinawa*, 439—43.
4. Inagaki, *Okinawa*, 216.
5. JM 135, 138.
6. Ibid., 138—40.
7. Ibid., 140; and Inagaki, *Okinawa*, 216.
8. JM 135, 140—42.
9. Ibid., 142—43.
10. Ibid., 133, 136—37; and Appleman, *Okinawa*, 451.
11. Appleman, *Okinawa*, 450.
12. Ibid., 451—54.
13. JM 135, 130.
14. Ibid., 139.
15. Ibid., 139—40.
16. JM 135, Book II, "Okinawa Operations Record of the 24th Division," 39, hereafter cited as JM 135—II.
17. Ibid., 40.
18. Ibid., 39—41.
19. Ibid., 33—34.
20. Ibid., 34.
21. Ibid., 35—36; and JM 135, 144.
22. Inagaki, *Okinawa*, 217.
23. Ibid., 218; and JM 135, 145—47.
24. *OHRS*, map 63, 596; and Appleman, *Okinawa*, Enclosed map 49.
25. JM·135, 143—44.
26. Ibid., 145—47.
27. Inagaki, *Okinawa*, 217.
28. JM 135, 146.
29. Ibid., 144; and Inagaki, *Okinawa*, 217.
30. Appleman, *Okinawa*, 458—59; and 77th ID, "G-2 Periodic Report," 22 June 1945, 4, and 25 June 1945, 1.
31. JM 135, 147.
32. Ibid., 147—48.
33. 77th ID, "G-2 Periodic Report," 25 June 1945, 3.

34. Ibid., 3—4.
35. JM 135—II, 40—41.
36. Ito interview; and JM 135, 150.
37. Appleman, *Okinawa*, 473—74; and 10th Army, "G-2 Summary," Inclosure 4, 1—2.
38. Inagaki, *Okinawa*, 220; and Appleman, *Okinawa*, 462, 467.
39. Nichols and Shaw, *Okinawa*, 303—4; and Appleman, *Okinawa*, 473—74.
40. Inagaki, *Okinawa*, 188.
41. Appleman, *Okinawa*, 489; and Nichols and Shaw, *Okinawa*, 56—57, 302—4.
42. 10th Army, "G-1 Periodic Reports," no. 13, 1—3. Appleman, using the same materials, arrived at similar numbers. See his *Okinawa*, 490.
43. See 10th Army, "G-1 Periodic Reports," no. 13, 1—3, and nos. 1 to 14.

Bibliography

Government Documents

U.S. Army. 10th Army. G-1 Section. "G-1 Periodic Reports, Numbers 1 to 14." Okinawa, 1 April 1945—7 July 1945.

U.S. Army. 10th Army, G-2 Section. "G-2 Weekly Summary, Number 2." Okinawa, 4 June 1945.

———. *Intelligence Monograph, Ryukyus Campaign.* Okinawa, 1945.

U.S. Army Forces Far East. Military History Section, ed. Japanese Monograph no. 135. *Okinawa Operations Record.* Washington, DC, 1949.

U.S. Army Forces, Pacific Ocean Areas. Assistant Chief of Staff, G-2 Section. "Test of Japanese Demolitions, Technical Intelligence Bulletin No. 16." Guam, June 1945.

U.S. Army Ground Forces, G-2 Section. "Information on Japanese Defensive Installations and Tactics." Washington, DC, August 1945.

U.S. Army. 77th Infantry Division. G-2 Section. "G-2 Periodic Report [Daily]." Okinawa, 25 May 1945.

———. "G-2 Summary—Okinawa from 27 April 1945 to 10 June 1945." Okinawa, June 1945.

U.S. Commander in Chief, Pacific, and Commander in Chief, Pacific Ocean Areas. "Searching Caves: A Summary of Techniques Developed at Okinawa, CINCPAC-CINCPOA Bulletin No. 189-45." Guam, August 1945.

U.S. Marine Corps. 6th Marine Division. "Sixth Marine Division on Okinawa Shima, G-2 Summary." Okinawa, August 1945.

U.S. War Department. Military Intelligence Division. *Japanese Tank and Antitank Warfare.* Washington, DC, 1945.

U.S. War Department. TM-E 30-480. *Handbook on Japanese Military Forces.* Washington, DC, 1 October 1944.

Interviews

Ito Koichi (former captain IJA). Interview with author. Tokyo, Japan, 28 November 1985.

Morimatsu Toshio (former captain IJA). Interview with author. Tokyo, Japan, November 1985.

Books

Appleman, Roy E., et al. *Okinawa: The Last Battle*. U.S. Army in World War II, 1948. Reprint. Washington, DC: Historical Division, Department of the Army, 1971.

Belote, James, and William Belote. *Typhoon of Steel: The Battle for Okinawa*. New York: Harper and Row, 1970.

Boei Kenkyujo senshishitsu, ed. *Okinawa homen rikugun sakusen, Senshi sosho* [Okinawa area infantry strategy, War History Series]. Vol 11. Tokyo: Asakumo shimbunsha, 1968.

Bradley, John H. *The Second World War: Asia and the Pacific*. West Point Military History Series. Wayne, NJ: Avery Publishing, 1984.

Coox, Alvin D. *Nomonhan: Japan Against Russia, 1939*. 2 vols. Stanford, CA: Stanford University Press, 1985.

Inagaki Takeshi. *Okinawa: higu no sakusen* [Okinawa: a strategy of tragedy]. Tokyo: Shinchosha, 1984.

Isely, Jeter A., and Philip A. Crowl. *The U.S. Marines and Amphibious War: Its Theory and Practice in the Pacific*. Princeton, NJ: Princeton University Press, 1951.

Leed, Eric J. *No Man's Land: Combat and Identity in World War I*. London: Cambridge University Press, 1979.

Mikami Masahiro. "62d Division Crisis and Commitment of the Bulk of 32d Army in the Northern Front." In *Okinawa Campaign, Data for MHX-85*, translated by Yanase Tokui. Tokyo: JGSDF Staff College, December 1985.

Nichols, Charles S., and Henry I. Shaw. *Okinawa: Victory in the Pacific*. Washington, DC: Historical Branch, G-3 Division, U.S. Marine Corps, 1955.

Nishimura Hitoshi. "Command and Staff Activities in the Offensive Operations on 4 May 1945." In *Okinawa Campaign, Date for MHX-85*, translated by Yanase Tokui. Tokyo: JGSDF Staff College, December 1985.

Rikusen-shi kenkyu fukyu kai, ed. [Land Warfare Research and Publicization Association, ed.] *Okinawa sakusen, Dainiji sekai taisen shi, Rikusen shishu* 9 (Okinawa strategy, history of World War II, land warfare history collection, vol. 9). Tokyo: Hara shobo, 1974 [1968].

Yahara Hiromichi. *Okinawa kessen* [Battle of Okinawa]. Tokyo: Yomiuri shimbunsha, 1972.

LEAVENWORTH PAPERS

1. *The Evolution of U.S. Army Tactical Doctrine, 1946—76*, Major Robert A. Doughty
2. *Nomonhan: Japanese-Soviet Tactical Combat, 1939*, by Dr. Edward J. Drea
3. *"Not War But Like War"; The American Intervention in Lebanon*, by Dr. Roger J. Spiller
4. *The Dynamics of Doctrine: The Changes in German Tactical Doctrine During the First World War*, by Captain Timothy T. Lupfer
5. *Fighting the Russians in Winter: Three Case Studies*, by Dr. Allen F. Chew
6. *Soviet Night Operations in World War II*, by Major Claude R. Sasso
7. *August Storm: The Soviet 1945 Strategic Offensive in Manchuria*, by Lieutenant Colonel David M. Glantz
8. *August Storm: Soviet Tactical and Operational Combat in Manchuria, 1945*, by Lieutenant Colonel David M. Glantz
9. *Defending the Driniumor: Covering Force Operations in New Guinea, 1944*, by Dr. Edward J. Drea
10. *Chemical Warfare in World War I: The American Experience, 1917—1918*, by Major Charles E. Heller, USAR
11. *Rangers: Selected Combat Operations in World War II*, by Dr. Michael J. King
12. *Seek, Strike, and Destroy: U.S. Army Tank Destroyer Doctrine in World War II*, by Dr. Christopher R. Gabel
13. *Counterattack on the Naktong, 1950*, by Dr. William Glenn Robertson
14. *Dragon Operations: Hostage Rescues in the Congo, 1964—1965*, by Major Thomas P. Odom
15. *Power Pack: U.S. Intervention in the Dominican Republic, 1965—1966*, by Dr. Lawrence A. Yates
16. *Deciding What Has to Be Done: General William E. DePuy and the 1976 Edition of FM 100—5, Operations*, by Major Paul H. Herbert
17. *The Petsamo-Kirkenes Operation: Soviet Breakthrough and Pursuit in the Arctic, October 1944*, by Major James F. Gebhardt
18. *Japan's Battle of Okinawa, April — June 1945*, by Dr. Thomas M. Huber

RESEARCH SURVEYS

1. *Amicicide: The Problem of Friendly Fire in Modern War*, by Lieutenant Colonel Charles R. Shrader
2. *Toward Combined Arms Warfare: A Survey of 20th-Century Tactics, Doctrine, and Organization*, by Captain Jonathan M. House
3. *Rapid Deployment Logistics: Lebanon, 1958*, by Lieutenant Colonel Gary H. Wade
4. *The Soviet Airborne Experience*, by Lieutenant Colonel David M. Glantz
5. *Standing Fast: German Defensive Doctrine on the Russian Front During World War II*, by Major Timothy A. Wray
6. *A Historical Perspective on Light Infantry*, by Major Scott R. McMichael
7. *Key to the Sinai: The Battles for Abu Ageila in the 1956 and 1967 Arab-Israeli Wars*, by Dr. George W. Gawrych